# The 50 Greatest Grand Prix Winners

**Neil Cowland**

How does one judge the fifty greatest of anything? Purely personal choices are open to many criticisms, and who can say one individual is greater than any other from a different era? Most sport contains human effort, either as an individual or within a team. Yet motor racing has the added complication of ever advancing technology and machinery. How would Moss have fared against Senna in a McLaren? Would Prost have beaten Fangio in a Mercedes? Would Villeneuve be quicker than Clark, Hill or Ascari? Such differences in technology over the years make it impossible to assess. In order to find the fifty greatest I have had to rely upon statistics rather than personal judgement.

Priority goes to drivers who have become World Champion, and these drivers are placed according to the number of times they have won the title. Any ties in world titles are settled by Grand Prix wins, and this second criterion helps place the non-World Champions according to their own tally of Grand Prix victories. I believe that this gives a reasonably good guide to a driver's greatness, although drivers such as Stirling Moss are not as high in my list of fifty greatest drivers as they deserve simply because they were not World Champion. Finally I have only included results since the FIA World Championship began in 1950 up until the end of the 1995 season. This means such greats as Nuvolari and Caracciola do not appear. Although I have attempted to check all references, if any mistakes have arisen I would be happy to hear about them in order to make any corrections for the next edition.

*Acknowledgements*
Firstly I am indebted to my family for nurturing a love of sport in me. My brother Alan, especially, has helped enliven either a cold October day at Brands, or a Grand Prix in July, with his infectious enthusiasm and knowledge. As well as my brother I must thank Paul Crewe, Steve Ing, Sean Freeman, Andrew Crombie, Andrew Kirk and Vince Brooks who have shared Grand Prix days and other motor racing occasions with me, providing great company as the countdown to the race begins. So far as the book is concerned I am very grateful to Champion Press for producing it, and Sporting Pictures (UK) Ltd and Doug Nye at the Goddard Picture Library for the photographs contained within it. I hope you enjoy it as much as I have enjoyed researching and writing it.

Neil Cowland, London

© Champion Press 1996

All rights reserved. No part of this publication may be reproduced, stored in a retrieval system, or transmitted, in any form or by any means without the prior written permission of the publisher, nor be otherwise circulated in any form of binding or cover other than that in which it is published and without a similar condition being imposed on the subsequent purchaser.

ISBN 1-898058-10-5

Printed and bound in Great Britain by the Ashi Press Ltd.
Champion Press
P.O. Box 284, Sidcup, Kent, DA15 8XX 0181-302-6446

Photographs © Sporting Pictures UK and the Goddard Picture Library

# 1

## Juan-Manuel Fangio

In life you must always try to be the best, but never believe you are. Perhaps I lost interest in trying. At first, motor racing had been a way of letting off steam. Then it became a passion and a career. It was both beautiful and wonderful, but it was just a period of my life.

*Juan-Manuel Fangio* was born on 24 June 1911 in Balcarce, Argentina. The son of an Italian immigrant stonemason, Fangio's character was shaped by honest hard work and loyal friendships. His first race was at Benito Juarez, when he raced under the assumed name of Rivadivia in an effort to avoid his father discovering his racing. When he was eventually found out, his father told him off for letting him find out from someone else. During the 1940s he became Argentinian champion twice, and when in 1950, the FIA instigated the first world championship, Fangio drove for Alfa Romeo. A year later he won his first world championship before signing for Maserati in 1952. He was runner-up in the championship in 1953, and after only two races of the next season, he changed to Mercedes Benz and proceeded to dominate the championship with six victories. He won the world title again in 1955, and the following year he moved to Ferrari. Although triumphant for a third consecutive season, he was generally unhappy and returned to Maserati to gain a fourth title. His greatest victory came in the German Grand Prix of 1957. After a long pit stop, and with just ten laps to go, he was trailing the Ferraris of Mike Hawthorn and Peter Collins by 48 seconds. Breaking the lap record nine times, he passed Collins on the penultimate lap and then overtook Hawthorn. The two of them battled it out to the line, where Fangio eventually won by 3.6 seconds, claiming his fifth title. It was later found that he had driven the final part of the race with a broken seat, holding himself in the cockpit with just his knees. Later he said, "I believe I was inspired that day. I never drove quite like that before, and I never drove quite like that again." Fangio retired in 1958 and became President of the Mercedes Benz subsidiary in Buenos Aires. On July 17 1995, aged 84, Fangio died of pneumonia after being dependent upon dialysis for several years because of kidney failure.

## World Champion

**1951**
**1954**
**1955**
**1956**
**1957**

## Grand Prix Wins

**1950**
Monaco
Belgium
France
**1951**
Switzerland
France
Spain
**1953**
Italy
**1954**
Argentina
Belgium
France
Germany
Switzerland
Italy
**1955**
Argentina
Belgium
Holland
Italy
**1956**
Argentina
Britain
Germany
**1957**
Argentina
Monaco
France
Germany

# 2

## Alain Prost

> "The simple fact is I loathe being expected to project a world champion image - whatever that is supposed to be - or being paraded as some kind of ideal. I am simply not built that way. I choose my own line and stick to it through thick and thin, in public and in private, on the track and off it. For me, the only genuinely important thing is to be honest with myself."

*Alain Prost.* "The Professor", was born on 24 February 1955, in St. Chamond and due to his modest background - his parents were unable to buy him a single-seater racing car - he enrolled with the best racing school in France, L'Ecole Winfield. He also decided to go to the track furthest from home, because of the wet condition of the local track at finals time. Prost's clear thinking came off and he won his final by a large margin, going on to clinch a Formula Renault drive and winning twelve out of the thirteen races. In 1979, he won the European F3 championship, and was signed for the McLaren F1 team. Although the McLaren was uncompetitive, Prost's performances attracted the expanding Renault team, and he joined France's national team for 1981. By the summer Prost had won three times and come second twice, but was under pressure to become his country's first world champion. The machinery would not quite get him there, and with a little bitterness he moved back to McLaren in 1984. His mood lightened within the team and although he lost out to team-mate Niki Lauda by half a point in 1984, he became world champion in the following two years. The arrival of Ayrton Senna in 1988 saw a great, and sometimes acrimonious, rivalry develop. The two best drivers of their time were now in the best car, and they won all but one of that year's Grands Prix, Senna emerging as champion. The next year Prost was champion before moving on to Ferrari, where he challenged Senna again for the world title until he was taken out by his rival at Suzuka. During 1991 the Ferrari was uncompetitive, and after taking a year out, Prost returned in a Williams to take his fourth title. His retirement at the end of that 1993 season left him with a record number of 51 Grands Prix wins. At the end of 1995 it seemed as if he may return to race a McLaren, but instead took up a post as technical adviser to the team.

**World Champion**
**1985, 1986**
**1989, 1993**

**Grand Prix Wins**
**1981**
France
Holland, Italy
**1982**
S. Africa, Brazil
**1983**
France, Belgium
Britain, Austria
**1984**
Brazil, San Marino
Monaco, Germany
Holland, European
Portugal
**1985**
Brazil, Monaco
Britain, Austria
Italy
**1986**
San Marino, Monaco
Austria, Australia
**1987**
Brazil, Belgium
Portugal
**1988**
Brazil, Monaco
Mexico, France
Portugal, Spain
Australia
**1989**
USA, France
Britain, Italy
**1990**
Brazil, Mexico
France, Britain
Spain
**1993**
South Africa
San Marino,
Spain
Canada, France
Britain, Germany

# 3
## Ayrton Senna

"I am a professional. I have responsibilities. But I am also a human being, and the values I have in my life are stronger than many other people's desires to influence or destroy those values."

*Ayrton Senna da Silva* was born in Sao Paulo on 21 March 1960. He began driving karts at the age of four and became the Pan-American kart champion in 1977, before moving to England in 1981 to race Formula Fords. Senna won the British FF1600, the British and European FF2000 championships, then won the British Formula 3 series. He joined the Toleman F1 team in 1984 and almost notched up his first win at Monaco in the rain-affected race which was stopped before half-distance. When he joined Toleman he told them that "...I will do everything for you. Every time I get in your car I will give 100% effort. But if I eventually decide that the car is not competitive, I will go to another team..." Which is precisely what he did. In 1985 he joined Lotus and won five races. Peter Warr - his boss at Lotus - described Senna as arguably the greatest racing driver of all time adding: "...His refusal to accept anything less than perfection in his quest to seek out the limits of his awesome ability motivated and captivated everyone in the team..." When he joined McLaren in 1988 he found a car and a team which could deliver the world championship to him. He was champion three times for McLaren, winning 35 races and starting on pole position a remarkable 46 times. It was during these years that his rivalry with Alain Prost intensified to almost dangerous levels as they battled it out on the track. Senna's refusal to be second best on the track and his ruthless devotion to the job, hid his private side. Here was a man who was fiercely loyal to his family and country. He had a very strong faith and gave an enormous amount of time and money to charitable concerns and was usually the first to visit injured drivers and to continue to check on their health. Senna joined Williams in 1994 but during the San Marino Grand Prix, on 1 May, he died when his car went off whilst leading at the Tamburello curve. The shock around the world was immense, and the Brazilian President declared three days of mourning to honour their national hero.

### World Champion
1988
1990
1991

### Grand Prix Wins

**1985**
Portugal, Belgium
**1986**
Spain, USA
**1987**
Monaco, USA
**1988**
San Marino
Canada
USA, Britain
Germany
Hungary
Belgium, Japan
**1989**
San Marino
Monaco, Mexico
Germany
Belgium, Spain
**1990**
USA, Monaco
Canada, Germany
Belgium, Italy
**1991**
USA, Brazil
San Marino
Monaco
Hungary
Belgium
Australia
**1992**
Monaco
Hungary, Italy
**1993**
Brazil, Europe
Monaco, Japan
Australia

# 4
## Jackie Stewart

" I believe that God gives all race drivers - at grand prix level anyway - a gift, in greater or lesser degrees. But there's so much more to it than just knowing how to work pedals and steer a wheel. You need the right mental attitude to channel your talent properly, get the most from it. "

*John Young Stewart*, the son of an amateur motorcycle racer, was born on 11 June 1939. After his brother Jimmy was seriously injured at Le Mans in 1954, young Jackie was persuaded to take up alternative sports. He was an excellent clay-pigeon marksman and became a member of the British team in 1959, just missing out on selection for the Olympics the following year. Stewart would have represented Great Britain in the 1964 Games, but by then he had started a motor racing career with the backing of his father and brother. Over the next few years his talent was noticed more and more as he was clocking faster times than established drivers. In 1965, he joined BRM alongside Graham Hill, and won an epic battle between the two to win his first Grand Prix at Monza. He had a disappointing year in 1966, but he almost won first time out at Indianapolis, his engine expiring with only twenty laps to go. After a heavy crash at the Belgian Grand Prix, Jackie took up the cause of driver safety, and became known for his outspoken views on this subject, which eventually led to improvements for the competitors. In 1968 he joined Ken Tyrrell's F1 team, which became the start of a great alliance culminating in three world titles. Stewart retired after becoming world champion in 1973, and would have raced in 100 grands prix if team-mate François Cevert had not been tragically killed in practice, leaving Jackie to withdraw in his memory. Since retirement, Stewart has been involved in promotional work and television, as well as following his son Paul's career, first as a driver, then helping him establish Paul Stewart racing. In early 1996, Jackie Stewart announced his intentions of racing his own grand prix team in the 1997 season.

## World Champion
**1969**
**1971**
**1973**

## Grand Prix Wins
**1965**
Italy
**1966**
Monaco
**1968**
Holland
Germany
USA
**1969**
South Africa
Spain
Holland
France
Britain
Italy
**1970**
Spain
**1971**
Spain
Monaco
France
Britain
Germany
Canada
**1972**
Argentina
France
Canada
USA
**1973**
South Africa
Belgium
Monaco
Holland
Germany

# 5

## Niki Lauda

" There's no point dwelling on one's success because the pleasure of success is in the winning of the race, not in talking about it afterwards. OK, so I won the championship three times. But what does it really mean? It's the next week that counts, the next race, or whatever. I've always believed that the only positive way to view life is to look forward, not back.... "

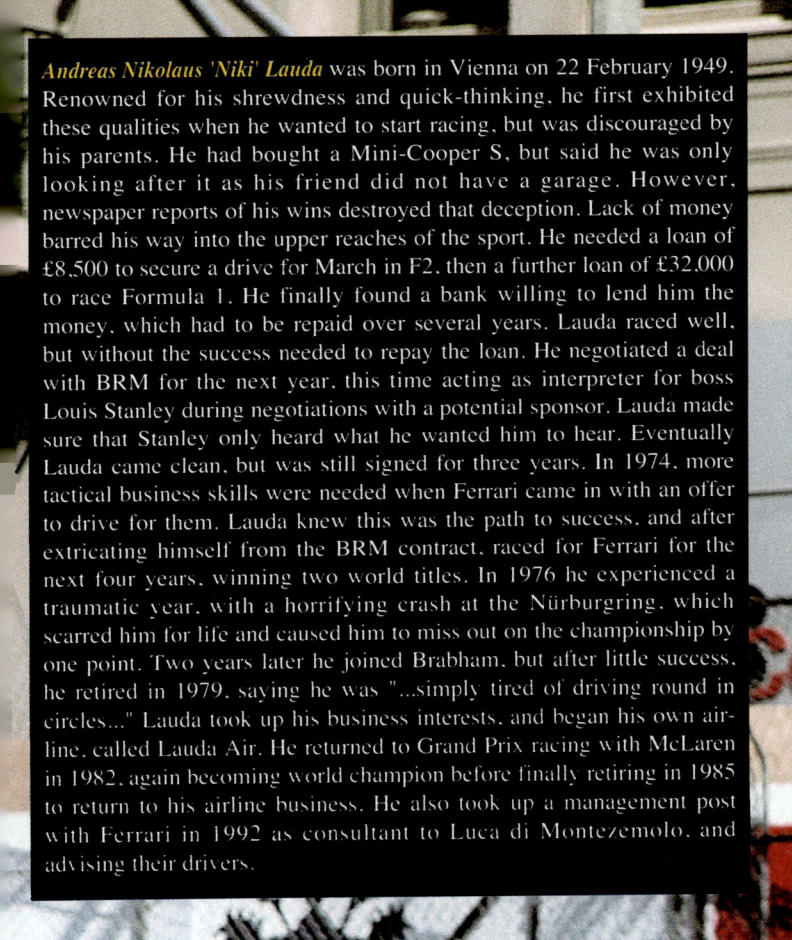

*Andreas Nikolaus 'Niki' Lauda* was born in Vienna on 22 February 1949. Renowned for his shrewdness and quick-thinking, he first exhibited these qualities when he wanted to start racing, but was discouraged by his parents. He had bought a Mini-Cooper S, but said he was only looking after it as his friend did not have a garage. However, newspaper reports of his wins destroyed that deception. Lack of money barred his way into the upper reaches of the sport. He needed a loan of £8,500 to secure a drive for March in F2, then a further loan of £32,000 to race Formula 1. He finally found a bank willing to lend him the money, which had to be repaid over several years. Lauda raced well, but without the success needed to repay the loan. He negotiated a deal with BRM for the next year, this time acting as interpreter for boss Louis Stanley during negotiations with a potential sponsor. Lauda made sure that Stanley only heard what he wanted him to hear. Eventually Lauda came clean, but was still signed for three years. In 1974, more tactical business skills were needed when Ferrari came in with an offer to drive for them. Lauda knew this was the path to success, and after extricating himself from the BRM contract, raced for Ferrari for the next four years, winning two world titles. In 1976 he experienced a traumatic year, with a horrifying crash at the Nürburgring, which scarred him for life and caused him to miss out on the championship by one point. Two years later he joined Brabham, but after little success, he retired in 1979, saying he was "...simply tired of driving round in circles..." Lauda took up his business interests, and began his own airline, called Lauda Air. He returned to Grand Prix racing with McLaren in 1982, again becoming world champion before finally retiring in 1985 to return to his airline business. He also took up a management post with Ferrari in 1992 as consultant to Luca di Montezemolo, and advising their drivers.

## World Champion

**1975**
**1977**
**1984**

## Grand Prix Wins

**1974**
Spain
Holland
**1975**
Monaco
Belgium
Sweden
France
USA
**1976**
Brazil
South Africa
Belgium
Monaco
Britain
**1977**
South Africa
Germany
Holland
**1978**
Sweden
Italy
**1982**
USA - West
Britain
**1984**
South Africa
France
Britain
Austria
Italy
**1985**
Holland

# 6
## Nelson Piquet

"The name of the game is to win by getting more points than anyone, not by outright winning. Some of the races I just finished second on purpose because I needed the six points in the hand more than the nine points which I might not have had."

## World Champion
*1981*
*1983*
*1987*

## Grand Prix Wins
*1980*
*USA - West*
*Holland*
*Italy*
*1981*
*Argentina*
*San Marino*
*Germany*
*1982*
*Canada*
*1983*
*Brazil*
*Italy*
*European*
*1984*
*Canada*
*USA - East*
*1985*
*France*
*1986*
*Brazil*
*Germany*
*Hungary*
*Italy*
*1987*
*Germany*
*Hungary*
*Italy*
*1990*
*Japan*
*Australia*
*1991*
*Canada*

**Nelson Souto Maior** was born in Rio de Janeiro on 17 August 1952. He was the son of a Brazilian politician who had been a good tennis player and wanted his son to follow suit. Piquet was sent to California at the age of 16 to develop his tennis, but fell in love with motor racing instead. His parents did not approve of his new sport, so he changed his name to Piquet (his mother's maiden name) to cover his karting and subsequent career. He notched up Brazilian karting honours, before moving to England, where he won the 1978 British F3 championship. This led to his first Grand Prix in an Ensign then further races in a private McLaren. Piquet was signed by the Brabham team in 1979 to partner Niki Lauda, and impressed everyone with his speed. When Lauda retired, Piquet became team leader, and under the team's guidance secured two world championships. Towards the end, he found that the Brabham was not as competitive as it used to be, and so in 1986 he signed for Williams. After enjoying total backing of his team-leader status at Brabham, he found the challenge of team-mate Nigel Mansell a problem, and cited that if Williams had backed him more, as the number one driver, Prost would not have won the title that year. The following year, consistent drives and tactical racing led Piquet to his third world crown, but with Williams due to lose its dominant Honda engine, Piquet moved to Lotus for the next season. Two fallow years forced him to join Benetton in 1990. He won a further three races over the next two years, but in 1992 he changed direction by taking up Indy Car racing. In practice for that year's Indianapolis 500, a bad accident saw Piquet suffer extensive foot injuries which ended his career.

# 7

## Jack Brabham

> " I look back on my career as one of absolute pleasure, along with a guilty feeling of selfishness in being separated from my family. They have supported me throughout my racing years, and the time has now come for me to throw off the increasing demands of a grand prix driver and spend more time with my family and my business interests. "

*John Arthur Brabham* was born in Hurstville, near Sydney, Australia on 2 April 1926, the son of a greengrocer who had emigrated from London in 1885. Jack became interested in mechanics at an early age, and worked in a garage when he left school. A visit to a Brisbane speedway track ignited his interest in motor sport and he took up racing. In 1954, Brabham bought himself a Cooper-Bristol, racing it in New Zealand and Australia and becoming firm friends with John Cooper, who invited him to work in his Surbiton factory to be employed on a rear-engined car. This enabled Jack to race against top class opposition - including Stirling Moss - in their front engined cars. In 1957 Brabham established himself in Grand Prix racing and two years later the Cooper was racing with great success. By the end of 1959, "Black Jack" (so called because of his five o'clock shadow) was world champion. He won a second title the following year, but in 1961 Formula 1 changed to 1.5 litre engines and the Cooper's dominance disappeared. However, their front-engined cars had changed the establishment's ideas about racing car design and Brabham decided to build his own cars, becoming the first man to win not only a race, but also the world championship, in his own make of car. Retiring in 1970 with a total of fourteen Grands Prix wins, he was a shrewd man who would speak rarely, and usually only in one word answers. The shy man later helped his sons in their racing careers, and was knighted for his services to sport in 1979.

## World Champion
*1959*
*1960*
*1966*

## Grand Prix Wins

*1959*
Monaco
Britain
*1960*
Holland
Belgium
France
Britain
Portugal
*1966*
France
Britain
Holland
Germany
*1967*
France
Canada
*1970*
South Africa

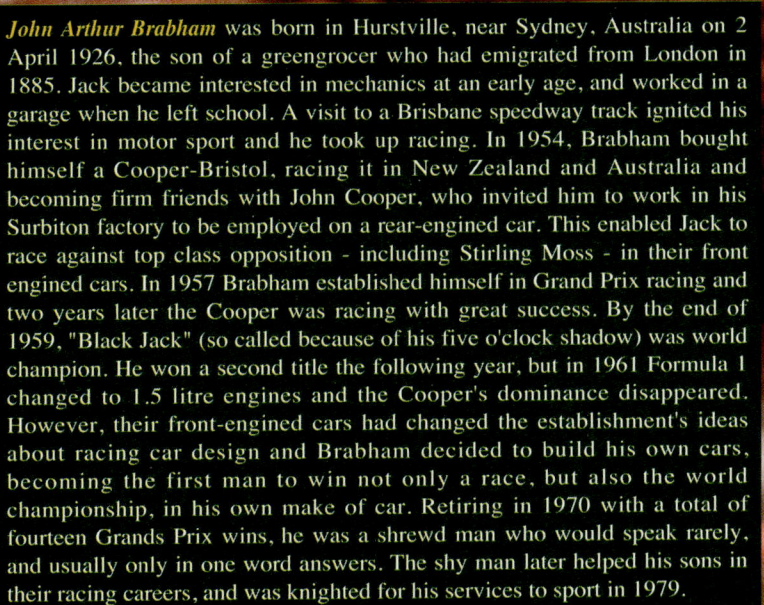

# 8

## Jim Clark

" I'm just beginning to wonder if I want to be World Champion. There will be so much fuss and drama. Farming is really my occupation, and racing just a hobby, although I make a serious effort at it. "

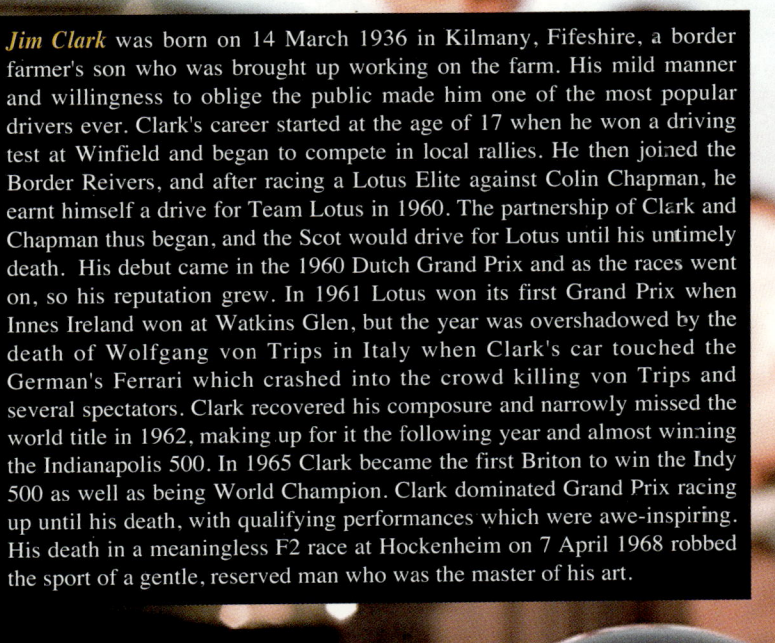

*Jim Clark* was born on 14 March 1936 in Kilmany, Fifeshire, a border farmer's son who was brought up working on the farm. His mild manner and willingness to oblige the public made him one of the most popular drivers ever. Clark's career started at the age of 17 when he won a driving test at Winfield and began to compete in local rallies. He then joined the Border Reivers, and after racing a Lotus Elite against Colin Chapman, he earnt himself a drive for Team Lotus in 1960. The partnership of Clark and Chapman thus began, and the Scot would drive for Lotus until his untimely death. His debut came in the 1960 Dutch Grand Prix and as the races went on, so his reputation grew. In 1961 Lotus won its first Grand Prix when Innes Ireland won at Watkins Glen, but the year was overshadowed by the death of Wolfgang von Trips in Italy when Clark's car touched the German's Ferrari which crashed into the crowd killing von Trips and several spectators. Clark recovered his composure and narrowly missed the world title in 1962, making up for it the following year and almost winning the Indianapolis 500. In 1965 Clark became the first Briton to win the Indy 500 as well as being World Champion. Clark dominated Grand Prix racing up until his death, with qualifying performances which were awe-inspiring. His death in a meaningless F2 race at Hockenheim on 7 April 1968 robbed the sport of a gentle, reserved man who was the master of his art.

## World Champion
**1963**
**1965**

## Grand Prix Wins

**1962**
Belgium
Britain
USA
**1963**
Belgium
Holland
France
Britain
Italy
Mexico
South Africa
**1964**
Holland
Belgium
Britain
**1965**
South Africa
Belgium
France
Britain
Holland
Germany
**1966**
USA
**1967**
Holland
Britain
USA
Mexico
**1968**
South Africa

# 9

## Michael Schumacher

> " I think I have mentally matured. I understand it all a lot better and I feel that everything in my own life is harmonious. I have no problems, no pressures, just motivations and ambitions. "

*Michael Schumacher* was born on 3 January 1969 at Hurth-Hermulheim, near Cologne in Germany, before moving the short distance to Kerpen, a town with a race track. His start in powered vehicles was not an auspicious one for a man who would later dominate Grand Prix racing in the mid-90s. At the first attempt Schumacher crashed his small go-kart into a lamppost. His parents thought it wiser if he took up racing on a track. This paid off in later years as he became German junior kart champion, runner-up in the junior world championships, then finally German senior kart champion by 1987. A year later Schumacher started in single-seater cars, winning the Formula Koenig championship at the first attempt, finishing the season with a dominant pole position and win at Hockenheim. Schumacher became German F3 champion in 1990, joining Jordan the following year, making his Grand Prix debut at Spa. He had already shown his talent on the world scene in the Mercedes Benz group C sports car team and after just one race for Jordan, Benetton realised the potential of the man and signed him amid much legal wrangling. Schumacher stayed with Benetton for the next four years, showing his great joy of racing with broad grins whenever he appeared on the podium. He secured his first Grand Prix win in 1992 at the same track on which he had made his debut, then went on to record a further eighteen wins for Benetton. Schumacher's first world title was marred by the death of Ayrton Senna, the man whom he felt confident would be World Champion that year. The Benetton team itself were found guilty of infringing FIA rules in some matters resulting in a disqualified win in Belgium and a subsequent two race ban. This set up a nail-biting finish to the season in Adelaide, when championship rivals Damon Hill and Schumacher collided, leaving the German as World Champion. Further clashes between the two rivals continued the following year, yet Schumacher became champion for the second time and with the help of Johnny Herbert, enabled Benetton to become the constructors champions for the first time. In 1995, Schumacher signed for Ferrari for a reputed $25 million over a period of two years.

### World Champion
*1994*
*1995*

### Grand Prix Wins
*1992*
*Belgium*
*1993*
*Portugal*
*1994*
*Brazil*
*Pacific*
*San Marino*
*Monaco*
*Canada*
*France*
*Hungary*
*Europe*
*1995*
*Brazil*
*Spain*
*Monaco*
*France*
*Germany*
*Belgium*
*Europe*
*Pacific*
*Japan*

# 10

## Graham Hill

> "You know the risks, you accept them. If man can't look at danger and still go on, man has stopped living. If the worst ever happens - then it means simply that I have been asked to pay the bill for the happiness of my life - without a moment's regret."

*Norman Graham Hill* was born on 15 February 1929, the son of a stockbroker who did not drive. Cars did not really come into Hill's life until 1953 when he tried a racing car at Brands Hatch, paying £1 for four laps. His great passion was rowing, where he was an oarsman for the London Rowing Club, whose colours would adorn his - and later his son's - racing helmets. He enjoyed success in the Grand Challenge Cup at Henley, and coached the Stuart Ladies Rowing Club to win the Head of the River race in successive years on two occasions, as well as meeting his wife Bette, who was in the team. This confidence in his coaching skill showed itself again when he offered his services as an instructor at the Brands Hatch racing school after those four paid laps. This, he thought, was a way into motor racing which he realised was what he really wanted to do, and he used his social skills to gain work and experience in and around cars. In 1955, Lotus held a test day and at the day's end employee Hill was allowed a quick run, promptly setting the second quickest time of the day. By 1958 he had driven for Lotus in an F1 race, but decided to join BRM in 1960. Two years later he won his first race and the world championship. He adapted well to becoming champion, showing the skills of an articulate speaker and raconteur which would become his trademark. By 1966 Hill had finished runner-up in the championship twice to Jim Clark and had won that year's Indianapolis 500. In 1967 he teamed up with Clark at Lotus. However the death of the Scotsman the following year left a huge cloud over the team and Hill succeeded in lifting it a little by bringing Lotus the world title that season. Hill broke both his legs at the US Grand Prix in 1969, only to return to a string of disappointing cars. The only highlight was his victory at Le Mans in 1972, becoming the first man to win the World Championship, the Indianapolis 500 and Le Mans. He retired in 1975 to set up his own F1 team, but died in an aeroplane accident on 31 November 1975.

## World Champion
1962
1968

## Grand Prix Wins
1962
Holland
Germany
Italy
South Africa
1963
Monaco
USA
1964
Monaco
USA
1965
Monaco
USA
1968
Spain
Monaco
Mexico
1969
Monaco

*Emerson Fittipaldi* was the first in a string of very successful Brazilian racing drivers. He was the youngest world champion and his longevity as a driver meant that he was still winning Indy Car races in the 1990s. He was born in Sao Paulo on 12 December 1946, the son of a motor racing journalist and it was natural that he and brother Wilson junior would take up the sport. By the age of 21, Emerson won the Brazilian Formula Vee championship as well as many other notable successes and decided to move to Europe. Fittipaldi won in Formula Fords and F3, and was signed by Lotus to race F2 in 1970. His debut came at the British Grand Prix, but following the death of Jochen Rindt later that year, he was put firmly in the limelight, going on to win the United States Grand Prix. By 1972, Fittipaldi's composure was sure enough to win the world championship in the remarkable Lotus 72. The following year the Lotus won seven races but because they were split between Fittipaldi and team mate Ronnie Peterson, the title went to Jackie Stewart. In 1974 Fittipaldi joined McLaren, winning the world title for the second time, including his home Grand Prix at Interlagos. He was a runner-up in 1975, leaving a record of first, second, first, second in the years between 1972 and 1975. In 1976 Fittipaldi shocked everyone by setting up his own team with the backing of Copersucar, the Brazilian sugar giant. However, successes were few, and in 1982 the team was wound up, prompting Fittipaldi to move to the United States to begin his successful Indy career. During his time in the States, he won the 1989 Indianapolis 500 and the Indy Car championship and a further Indy 500 win in 1993.

## World Champion
**1972**
**1974**

## Grand Prix Wins
**1970**
USA
**1972**
Spain
Belgium
Britain
Austria
Italy
**1973**
Argentina
Brazil
Spain
**1974**
Brazil
Belgium
Canada
**1975**
Argentina
Britain

# 12
## Alberto Ascari

> **Like my father, like all those who embrace this career, I only obey my instinct: without it, I would not know how to live, I would not succeed in making any sense of my days.**

*Alberto Ascari* was the fastest starter of all. This highly superstitious man is regarded by many as one of the greatest drivers of all time, and indeed Fangio announced after Ascari's death: "I have lost my greatest opponent." Ascari was born on 13 July 1918 in Milan, the son of one of Italy's most successful drivers. Ascari acquired father Antonio's speed as well as a double-edged personality: a calm and confident-looking exterior hiding a dark inner temperament. This was not all he shared with his father, for they both died at the wheel of a car aged 36 and on the 26th day of the month. Despite the death of his father, Alberto became a works rider for the Italian motor cycle team, Bianchi. Although he was very successful on two wheels, he harboured a deep passion for cars, and in 1940 Ascari approached Enzo Ferrari and became one of the first two drivers to race a Ferrari. In 1950 the first world championship took place with Ascari driving for Ferrari. He could have been the first man to win a Grand Prix for the Italian team, but showed his team spirit by declining to take over Froilan Gonzalez's car, leaving the Argentinian to score that first Grand Prix win. Ascari's decision to turn down his team leader's right also cost him the championship itself, but in 1952 and 1953 under two-litre F2 regulations Ascari became world champion in a Ferrari 500. In 1955 he survived one of the most famous accidents in motor racing history. Little knowing that he was about to take the lead - as Moss had just retired from the race - his car ploughed into Monaco's harbour. Ascari was taken to hospital with a broken nose, but discharged himself in order to drive a Ferrari 750 sports car four days later. After a few laps in the car, Ascari crashed inexplicably and was killed instantly. Previously, he had confided with Fangio at Monaco, "My game is going wrong - the star is setting."

**World Champion**
1952
1953

**Grand Prix Wins**
1951
Germany
Italy
1952
Belgium
France
Britain
Germany
Holland
Italy
1953
Argentina
Holland
Belgium
Britain
Switzerland

# 13

## Nigel Mansell

> **"** Whenever I get into a car I will commit myself and do everything in my power to achieve the best possible result. All things being equal that will mean going for a win.

*Nigel Mansell* was born in Upton-on-Severn on 8 August 1954. It was with the help of father Eric that Mansell took his first steps into motor racing. Originally, he worked at Lucas Aerospace before taking up karts and with encouragement from his father, he moved up into Formula Fords, winning his first event. Later that same year, 1976, Mansell broke his neck at Brands Hatch. The medical experts said his racing career was over, but Mansell thought differently. He progressed into F3, where he had to sell his house, take out a large overdraft and with the support of his wife Rosanne, write letters to potential sponsors, all to get a few races. Success had to come with debts and promises hanging over them, and in 1979 the big break came. Despite a crushed vertebra from a recent race, Mansell responded to a call from Colin Chapman to test a Lotus F1. The doctors told him to rest his back for two to three months, but Mansell had given it only a week. His decision paid off and he impressed Chapman, who offered him a testing contract. His engineering background helped the mechanics, and it was not long before Mansell started his first Grand Prix, although it resulted in first degree burns when petrol was spilt on him before the race. In 1984 he joined Williams and by the following year he had won his first Grand Prix in front of a patriotic crowd at Brands Hatch. He would dominate racing in Britain and attracted a fanatical army of spectators, but the world championship eluded him. Spectacular tyre failure in Australia in 1986 and a crash in Japan the following year ended his hopes in the 1980s. Finally, in 1992, after a record nine wins in a season, he achieved his ambition. He moved to Indy cars in 1993, promptly winning that title, becoming the first man to win both the F1 World Championship and the Indy car titles in successive seasons. But his return to Grand Prix racing was not as successful, retiring after only a few races in a McLaren in 1995.

## World Champion
*1992*

## Grand Prix Wins

*1985*
European
South Africa

*1986*
Belgium
Canada
France
Britain
Portugal

*1987*
San Marino
France
Britain
Austria
Spain
Mexico

*1989*
Brazil
Hungary

*1990*
Portugal

*1991*
France
Britain
Germany
Italy
Spain

*1992*
South Africa
Mexico
Brazil
Spain
San Marino
France
Britain
Germany
Portugal

*1994*
Australia

# 14

## Alan Jones

" I never thought that I wanted to race cars as an ambition - I just thought it would be natural that I should, just part of growing up. "

*Alan Jones*, the son of Stan Jones, a successful driver in Australia just after World War Two, caught the racing bug early. Born in Melbourne on 2 November 1946, Alan started out in karts and gradually built up his career until in 1964 the family car business collapsed and his father had a stroke. Moving to England, Alan and wife Beverly became street traders in VW Caravanettes before running a boarding house. Alan kept racing on a very tight budget until in 1975 Harry Stiller, a wealthy enthusiast who had helped Jones in Formula Atlantic racing, bought a Hesketh and ran it privately with Jones driving it. After four races Stiller's money ran out, but Jones had impressed Graham Hill enough, who offered him a drive in his team. Hill's fatal air crash, however, meant that Jones was soon out of a job again. He drove for Surtees in 1976 before signing for Shadow and winning their first-ever Grand Prix. Alan joined perennial survivor Frank Williams in 1978 and with each other's help, and the designs of Patrick Head, the Williams outfit emerged to become world leaders. After a reasonably successful year with the FW06, Head introduced his FW07 machine in 1979, the car that would take Jones to his world championship. It won its first race in Britain, with team-mate Clay Regazzoni taking over from the dominant Jones when he had to retire from the race. Jones then won the next three races in succession, winning a fourth later on that season. In 1980 Jones won the world championship, and with new team-mate Carlos Reutemann, Williams bagged the constructors' title. Mechanical problems robbed Jones of another title in 1981 and he retired at the end of the year, returning for Arrows then Haas-Lola, but without the competitive edge he had enjoyed at Williams.

**World Champion**
*1980*

**Grand Prix Wins**

*1977*
**Austria**
*1979*
**Germany**
**Austria**
**Holland**
**Canada**
*1980*
**Argentina**
**France**
**Britain**
**Canada**
**USA - East**
*1981*
**USA - West**
**Las Vegas**

*Mario Andretti* was one of the most versatile drivers throughout his racing career. He was born on 28 February 1940 in Montona, Italy, where Mario, his twin brother Aldo and his family spent the first seven years of his life in a displaced person's camp. After this they moved to Lucca, where the brothers found they liked racing cars. In 1955, the family emigrated to Nazareth in Pennsylvania, where the twins worked in their uncle's garage and visited the Nazareth speedway. It was there that their Italian racing experiences saw Aldo win the first race and Mario follow it up the next week. By 1963 Mario was an established driver, whereas Aldo had stopped racing following a fractured skull. A year later Mario broke into USAC racing and in 1965 won the first of three championships in the 1960's (the others being in 1966 and 1969). In 1967 he won the Daytona 500 and two years later the Indianapolis 500. When he became F1 world champion in 1978 he was the first man to win the F1 world title, the Indianapolis and Daytona. His rise to world champion status began in 1968 when he started from pole position in his first Grand Prix at Watkins Glen. He drove for Lotus, March, Ferrari and Parnelli before re-joining Lotus for the most important phase in his career. After much testing by Mario, the Lotus became a competitive car again and the ground effect revolution started by Colin Chapman's Lotus 78s and 79s saw Andretti clinch the driver's crown after the tragic death of his supportive team-mate Ronnie Peterson at Monza. The other teams caught up with Lotus's lead in 1979 and 1980, and after an unsuccessful switch to Alfa Romeo and a few guest races, he left for Indy car racing once more, where he established himself as a front runner alongside his son Michael and nephew John, becoming CART champion in 1984. He retired from Indy car racing in 1994.

**World Champion**
*1978*

**Grand Prix Wins**
*1971*
South Africa
*1976*
Japan
*1977*
USA - West
Spain
France
Italy
*1978*
Argentina
Belgium
Spain
France
Germany
Holland

# 16

## James Hunt

> "The kick was in the striving to achieve. I was born competitive and it is the challenge of trying to win that has always turned me on. It could have been anything. That it was racing was purely co-incidental."

## World Champion
*1976*

## Grand Prix Wins
*1975*
Holland
*1976*
Spain
France
Germany
Holland
Canada
USA - East
*1977*
Britain
USA - East
Japan

*James Simon Wallis Hunt* was born on 29 August 1947, in Belmont, Surrey, the son of a London stockbroker. Hunt's education included prep school at Wellington College, whose colours he wore on his racing helmet. However, he received no financial help from his father when he decided to become a racing driver, and he had to find a number of jobs including labouring, night porter and van driver in order to build himself a racing mini which later proved to be hopelessly uncompetitive. Undeterred, Hunt won his first race in 1968 in a Formula Ford Russell Alexis. His progress through the ranks of F3 earnt him the nickname of 'Hunt the Shunt'. After driving for March in F3, he agreed to join Lord Alexander Hesketh who had decided to enter motor racing. In 1973 Hunt set his sights on the European F2 championship, but after writing off the Surtees in testing, Hesketh decided to enter Grand Prix racing. The fun-loving team with the playboy image did well in their inaugural season, but after a disappointing following year, they secured their historic first and only win in 1975 at Zandvoort before Hesketh pulled out of Formula One. Hunt joined McLaren in 1976 and won the world championship by a single point following some excellent drives and the accident to Niki Lauda. Hunt again drove well the next year, but without the same degree of success and in 1979 he joined Wolf. However, ground effect cars had taken too much of the driver's role away for Hunt's liking and he retired from the sport at Monaco. He returned to motor racing, first as Marlboro's adviser to their drivers, then as a commentator for BBC television. There his outspoken comments on drivers' antics were the perfect foil for the excitable Murray Walker. Hunt's death on 15 June 1993 from a heart attack was a shock to racing fans the world over, as he had become part of the British way of life and added a new dimension to motor racing.

# 17

## Jody Scheckter

> " I think I've had enough of driving. I did ten years, I did what I wanted to. At the beginning I thought I was the fastest driver in the world. At the end I thought I was the cleverest driver. "

*Jody Scheckter* was born in East London, South Africa on 29 January 1950. His rise to F1 was a very rapid one. He trained as an apprentice in his father's garage with racing as just a hobby, but in early 1971 he entered the Sunshine Series of Formula Ford and won it, earning a racing trip to England. After a few months of FF1600 and F3, he was given a drive in a works McLaren in the 1971 US Grand Prix. He had a steady year in F2 the following season, before hitting the headlines in 1973 after causing a multiple crash on the first lap of the British Grand Prix. His skills, rather than crashes, were noted by Ken Tyrrell who ironed out the reckless side of Scheckter when he signed him for 1974. The pair were to enjoy considerable success over the next three years. In 1975, he secured an emotional win in his home Grand Prix and the following year drove the revolutionary P34 six-wheeled car to a win at Anderstorp with team-mate Patrick Depailler completing a one-two. Seeing no potential for the six-wheeler, Scheckter joined the new Wolf team in 1977 and promptly won in their debut Grand Prix. He was runner-up in the world championship that year, and after a poor 1978 he joined Ferrari to realise his ambition of becoming world champion in 1979. His year of being world champion was not a successful one with the new Ferrari T5 not able to keep up with the opposition. Scheckter retired with great dignity at the end of the year and set up a business with his wife in Atlanta, specialising in high-tech security systems.

## World Champion
### 1979

## Grand Prix Wins
### 1974
Sweden
Britain
### 1975
South Africa
### 1976
Sweden
### 1977
Argentina
Monaco
Canada
### 1979
Belgium
Monaco
Italy

# 18

## Denny Hulme

> " I haven't done as well in society, maybe as I ought to have done. I know the people I really have to know - which is about three - but I don't like small talk and I haven't time for people who just sit down and talk about nothing, putting on as big a front as they can. No way. "

*Denis Clive Hulme's* characteristics were much the same as his father's. During World War Two at Anzio, Clive Hulme single-handedly attacked an enemy machine gun nest, subsequently winning the Victoria Cross. These family characteristics enabled Denny Hulme to become single-mindedly successful and dedicated to his job and those around him. He was born on 18 June 1936 in Nelson, South Island, New Zealand. An example of Denny's courage was in 1970 whilst driving McLaren's Indy car. Fuel had spilt on to his hands and ignited whilst he was driving at 200mph. For a year he was unable to read newspapers without sustaining cuts to his palms. In 1963 Hulme joined Jack Brabham's team as a mechanic and was able to prepare a car for himself as well as do other duties. He drove his first F1 race at Karlskoga, where he finished fourth, as well as driving the team's truck to and from the race. In 1965 he scored his first Grand Prix win and a year later he replaced Dan Gurney as Brabham's team-mate. The Brabham-Repco was a great success, as Jack Brabham took the title that year and Hulme won the following year. In 1968 Hulme joined fellow Kiwi Bruce McLaren's team and as well as racing in Grands Prix with three wins, he raced McLaren's car in the Can-Am series, also winning three times. The following year he was runner-up to McLaren in the Can-Am championship after five victories. In 1970 the death of Bruce McLaren devastated Hulme, but he never let it show in his driving, clinching that year's Can-Am title. His success on both sides of the Atlantic had brought him fame, but being shy and reserved, he hated the speeches that came with success. In 1991 he was awarded the OBE, and although he retired from F1 in 1974, he continued to race sports cars, trucks, and touring cars. He died from an apparent heart attack during the Bathurst 1000 kilometres on 4 October 1992. The strong man of racing had died where he had achieved so much success - behind the wheel.

## World Champion
*1967*

## Grand Prix Wins
*1967*
**Monaco**
**Germany**
*1968*
**Italy**
**Canada**
*1969*
**Mexico**
*1972*
**South Africa**
*1973*
**Sweden**
*1974*
**Argentina**

# 19

## Jochen Rindt

> " It is my expression of art to drive a car perfectly on a circuit; to be in complete control. "

*Karl Jochen Rindt* was born in Mainz-am-Rhein, Germany on 18 April 1942. He always considered himself an Austrian however, as he moved to Graz at the age of one when his father, a wealthy spice-mill owner and his mother, a lawyer, were killed in a bombing raid. For his 18th birthday his grandfather bought him a car which was entered for rallies and hill-climbs. When his grandfather died, he persuaded his grandmother to buy him a race-prepared Alfa Romeo and with it he won his first major race at Aspen in 1962. By 1964 Rindt was determined to race in F2 and sold his family spice mill and his own cars to buy a Brabham BT10. Over the years F2 proved to be a happy hunting ground as Rindt took on the Grand Prix stars who competed in both F2 and F1 in those days. In F1 Rindt was often unlucky after making his debut in the 1964 Austrian Grand Prix and didn't win a race until five years later when he crossed the line first at Watkins Glen. During 1969 Rindt had a string of unlucky failures when it looked as if he would finally secure that first win. However, even after his initial victory, there was open feuding between a frustrated Rindt and Lotus team boss Colin Chapman. Jack Brabham tried to sign Rindt into the team that the Austrian had enjoyed driving for previously, but with little success as the Lotus money and resources were really too good to turn down. Furthermore, in the development stage was the remarkable Lotus 72, so Rindt re-signed for Lotus. Rindt and the 72 were virtually unbeatable throughout 1970. With a large points lead the Austrian came to Monza. In an attempt to get more speed, he took some of the aerodynamic aids off the Lotus. In practice he crashed at 100mph and suffered severe injuries from which he died. He had, though, amassed enough points to win the world championship posthumously.

**World Champion**
*1970*

**Grand Prix Wins**
*1969*
USA
*1970*
Monaco
Holland
France
Britain
Germany

# 20

## John Surtees

> ❝ I look upon racing as a competitive thing. You're competing with someone and you have to go to a venue somewhere to do it. Frankly, all the other business, the pomp and the ceremony leaves me cold. I did my time in motorcycling, achieved what I wanted to achieve, and switched off. I did my time in cars, and I have to say that I didn't achieve all my ambitions there, but I had to compromise. ❞

*John Surtees* the son of successful racer and garage-owner Jack Surtees, was born on 11 February 1934 at Tatsfield in Surrey. After serving an apprenticeship with Vincent-HRD in Stevenage, he went on to carve out a great motor-cycle career which saw him take seven world championships for MV Augusta. He made his car racing debut in 1959 when Augusta did not make any bikes available for racing in Britain. Surtees was invited by Colin Chapman to drive in grands prix which did not clash with his motor-cycle commitments. He enjoyed successful races in Britain and Portugal that year, and by the end of 1961 he had stopped motor-cycle racing to concentrate solely on cars. In 1963 he signed for Ferrari, after two largely unsuccessful seasons with Cooper and Lola. He then won the 1963 German Grand Prix at the Nürburgring, the first Ferrari win for two years. A year later Surtees won the championship, thus becoming the first man to be world champion on both two and four wheels. After sporadic success over the next six years, with Ferrari, Cooper, Honda and BRM, Surtees decided to start up his own team in 1970. Team Surtees raced F5000 and F1 with some success, then solely focused on Formula One, achieving their best result with a fourth place from Vittorio Brambilla in the 1977 Belgian Grand Prix. Surtees retired from driving in 1973, to concentrate on running his own team, but financial problems over several years finally saw the team finish competitive racing. In 1978 Surtees was hospitalised but he met a ward sister who would later become his wife. After recovering, Surtees and his wife moved to a Kent country house, surrounded by the motor cycles and Surtees F1 cars that had formed his career.

**World Champion**
*1964*

**Grand Prix Wins**
*1963*
Germany
*1964*
Germany
Italy
*1966*
Belgium
Mexico
*1967*
Italy

## 21

## Nino Farina

> **❝** Being passed by you (Tazio Nuvolari) and following your car is a true lesson in itself, and every time I follow you around the course, I learn something new. **❞**

*Giuseppe 'Nino' Farina* was born on 30 October 1906 in Turin, Italy. His father was the eldest of the brothers who founded the Pinafarina Car Coachbuilding Company, and as well as winning three consecutive Italian championships from 1937 through to 1939 he became the first official World Champion in 1950. Even though he was a successful man, he hated the publicity and refused to have his photograph taken at home, partly because his wife disapproved of his racing activities. Farina started driving at the age of nine, but did not compromise his studies which culminated with a doctorate of engineering. He began competition driving in a 1500 Alfa Romeo in the 1932 Aosta-Grand St. Bernard hill climb. It was not a successful start as he was involved in a crash which resulted in a broken shoulder and facial cuts. His successes came much later with Alfa Romeos and he enjoyed victories both before and after the Second World War with them. In 1947 he left Alfa Romeo after a disagreement with the management, but re-joined them in 1950 for the initial World Championship after their three top drivers had all been killed. Farina's win in 1950 was followed up with fourth place to Fangio the following year. He then moved to Ferrari in 1952 where he stayed until his retirement in 1955, finally succumbing to the pain of burns sustained at Monza the previous year. However, his arms-stretched-out style was remembered and copied by other drivers as the definitive style to go racing with. In retirement, he became a Jaguar importer for Italy, before becoming the main agent for Alfa Romeo. On 30 June 1966, on his way to the French Grand Prix, he lost control of his Lotus Cortina in the Savoy Alps near Chambéry and crashed into a telegraph pole, dying instantly.

## World Champion
### 1950

## Grand Prix Wins
### 1950
**Britain
Switzerland
Italy**
### 1951
**Belgium**
### 1953
**Germany**

**22**

" Let's face it, we're just whores aren't we? We'll turn up and do our stuff for anyone, if the money's right. "

*Keke Rosberg*

*Keijo Erik 'Keke' Rosberg* was born on 6 December 1948, in Solna near Stockholm, Sweden, where his father, Lasse, was studying for veterinary exams. After qualifying, the family moved back to Lapinjarvi in their native Finland. Rosberg's early successes were in Formula Vee racing, but he really burst onto the racing scene at Silverstone in 1978 during the International Trophy race. This was only his second race in an F1 car, but he piloted his Theodore through the wet conditions that had already claimed the top names of Grand Prix racing, such as Lauda, Hunt and Peterson. By 1981, after an unsuccessful time in the Copersucar-Fittipaldi team, Rosberg was looking for either a drive in a competitive team or a return to Can-Am racing in North America. However, in November he received a phone call from Frank Williams, wanting him to replace Alan Jones, and now with a competitive car Rosberg was finally on the way. In 1982, when a crash at Hockenheim eliminated leader Didier Pironi from the title race, it looked like Rosberg would become the only driver to become world champion without winning a Grand Prix. However, a victory late in the season saw him beat John Watson to the championship. Although he did not add to that world title, he continued to put in some stunning performances both in races and in practice. This included a moment of drama at Silverstone in 1985 when he dropped his cigarette on the concrete, ground it out with his heel and said, "OK, let's do it." He then set the fastest ever practice lap in a grand prix at an average speed of 160.925mph. He looked to McLaren in 1986 to help him to another world title, only to see team-mate Alain Prost take it instead. After retiring from grands prix, Rosberg took up sports car racing then drove in the German touring car championship. He ran his own team in touring cars before retiring from competitive driving in 1995.

## World Champion
*1982*

## Grand Prix Wins
*1982*
Switzerland
*1983*
Monaco
*1984*
Dallas
*1985*
USA
Australia

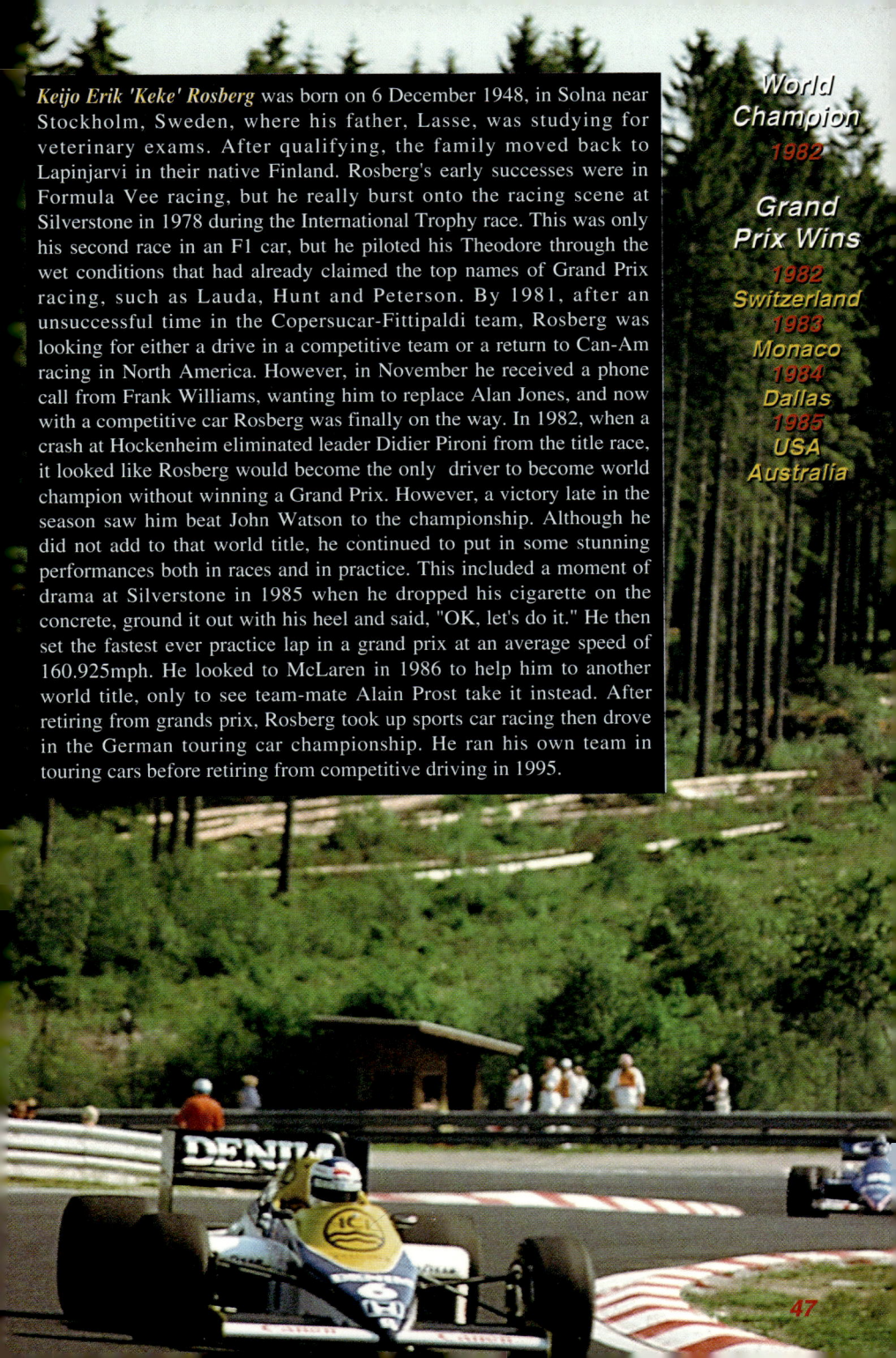

# 23

## Mike Hawthorn

> Grand prix racing is a calculated risk accepted by those who take part in it. No regulations could be drawn up which would guarantee safety. If you take away the normal hazards of motor racing you take away the reasons for going motor racing - and this applies to any venture into the comparative unknown.

*John Michael Hawthorn* was born 10 April 1929 at Mexborough, Yorkshire, the son of Leslie Hawthorn who took a partnership in a garage business in Farnham in 1931 principally so that he was near to Brooklands to pursue his motorcycle racing. Young Mike Hawthorn grew up with racing in his blood and progressed through bikes to cars. In 1952, he had a test drive in F2 Connaughts and an HWM. However, when the HWM drive went to future best friend Peter Collins, Hawthorn realised that he needed a car and a family friend helped to enter him in a Cooper-Bristol. On Easter Monday 1952, at Goodwood, Hawthorn beat Fangio who was driving in a similar car, and finished second to Gonzalez, receiving great press reviews. A year later he signed for Ferrari and notched up his finest win where he out-sprinted Fangio in the final straight at the Reims circuit. Early in 1954 he sustained serious burns during the Syracuse Grand Prix just after his father was killed in a road accident. After winning his second Grand Prix, he decided to leave Ferrari and join the British Vanwall team so that he could be near the family garage. Later that year saw unwelcome intrusions into Hawthorn's private life when he was accused of racing rather than doing his National Service. However, a kidney complaint that would have meant it unlikely that Hawthorn would live on after middle age proved to be the real reason for him missing a military interlude. In 1955 he gained success at Le Mans which was overshadowed by his involvement in the catastrophe that saw Pierre Levegh crash into the crowd and kill eighty people. Hawthorn re-joined Ferrari in 1957, and became Britain's first world champion the following year, beating Stirling Moss by one point, but losing his best friend Peter Collins in the German Grand Prix that same season. The pair had shared endless pranks and adventures on and off the track, so with the death of Collins and so many other colleagues, he decided to retire at the end of that season. Ironically, on 22 January 1959 the world champion lost his life on the Guildford bypass after seeing, then deciding to race, Rob Walker, the F1 team owner. He skidded and crashed into a tree, dying instantly.

**World Champion**
*1958*

**Grand Prix Wins**
*1953*
*France*
*1954*
*Spain*
*1958*
*France*

# 24

## Phil Hill

" When I think back on it all, it really does seem crazy to be so obsessed with that occupation. I had a lot of happy times with Ferrari and in racing generally, but I would have liked to have been more mature across the board throughout my career - but then if that happened I probably would have had more sense than to be a racing driver in the first place! "

*Philip Toll Hill junior* was born in Miami on 20 April 1927. He moved to Santa Monica near Los Angeles, when his father became Head Postmaster. In the late 1940s California was the centre of the sports car boom and Hill was able to exploit his skills as a racing driver. After a spell in England as a Jaguar trainee, he returned to America with a Jaguar XK120 and drove it with great success. After driving well in a Ferrari, he was recommended to Enzo Ferrari to drive in the works team at Le Mans in 1956 and 1957. Throughout his career Hill enjoyed considerable success driving sports cars, winning the Argentine 1000km, the Sebring 12hours, and Le Mans. He made his Grand Prix debut at Reims in 1958, in the same race that saw the end of Fangio's career. In that race Hill drove a Maserati, but later drove for Ferrari in Germany, where he teamed up with von Trips, Collins and Mike Hawthorn. In the final Grand Prix of the season in Casablanca, Hill let Hawthorn pass him to secure second place in the race and deprive the winner, Stirling Moss, of the championship by one point. Hill's first win was at Monza in 1960 when a lot of the British teams withdrew because the banking on the circuit was considered unsafe. In 1961, driving the dominant Ferrari 156, Hill was a consistent finisher in the points and became world champion after his third Grand Prix win, but it was not a happy victory as Hill's team-mate, Wolfgang von Trips, looked set to become champion himself until he crashed and died. The Ferraris were not so quick the following year and after many arguments with team owner Enzo Ferrari, he left to join ATS, then moved to Cooper, before finishing his career in a second-hand BRM. Hill continued sports car racing for two more years before forgetting to renew his international competitions licence, which forced his retirement. Hill moved back to Santa Monica after it was discovered he had been suffering from stomach ulcers for some time. He decided to concentrate on his old car restoration business and his collection forms one of America's best-known car museums.

**World Champion**
*1961*

**Grand Prix Wins**
*1960*
*Italy*
*1961*
*Belgium*
*Italy*

**25**

## Stirling Moss

> " I have always enjoyed my motor racing ... and although the world title is still something that I would like to win, I learned a valuable lesson; that if I don't, there is nothing much I can do about it. "

*Stirling Crauford Moss* was born on 17 September 1929 to Alfred and Aileen Moss, a prosperous dentist and part-time amateur racing driver, and a lady rally driver. Stirling might have become a show jumper or taken a job in the catering trade but he turned to racing with a hill climb in Brighton in 1948. In 1951, his form in F3 attracted the attention of Ferrari, who offered Moss a works drive in the non-championship Bari Grand Prix. However, when he turned up he found that someone else was driving instead, and from then on Moss took great delight at beating the Ferraris. By 1954, he was driving for Maserati, but after efforts from his father to convince Mercedes team manager Alfred Neubauer to let Stirling race for them, he then partnered Fangio in Grands Prix and sports car races. The sight of the pair seemingly joined together became a familiar one, earning the nickname of '*The Train.*' Moss was fiercely patriotic and only drove for overseas teams when there were no British ones able to compete, until in 1957 he joined Vanwall. Moss was beaten to the 1958 world title by Mike Hawthorn in the final race of the season when he protested Hawthorn's disqualification in Portugal. At Goodwood in 1962 he suffered a serious accident which led to his retirement. He tested a sports car during the following year, but decided to stay retired. Stirling Moss was a great British hero, and still drove in demonstration races in later years.

## Grand Prix Wins

**1955**
Britain
**1956**
Monaco
Italy
**1957**
Britain
(shared with Tony Brooks)
Pescara
Italy
**1958**
Argentina
Holland
Portugal
Morocco
**1959**
Portugal
Italy
**1960**
Monaco
USA
**1961**
Monaco
Germany

# 26

## Damon Hill

> "You know, I've got children and houses and mortgages and all that stuff. So I think that a World Championship's not much of a thing to worry about, is it?"

*Damon Graham Devereux Hill* was born 17 September 1960 in London. Being the son of a famous father can be daunting, but when your father is as big a legend as Graham Hill, then there is even more to live up to. The young Hill's first drive in a car was at the age of five when he would drive the family's old car around, yet it was racing bikes that first attracted his attention. Whilst at Silverstone, he saw someone riding a 50cc Monkey bike and he was bought one of these by his father before going on to race larger bikes when he was older. At the age of fourteen, Graham Hill was killed in a plane crash, but Damon's resolve to become a racing driver remained undiminished. In 1984, he won forty bike races in a season, but by then he had driven in Formula Ford. Although his debut was a disaster, he went on to win his first Formula Ford race at Brands Hatch at the end of that same year. The following year he won six races and finished third in the Esso FF1600 championship, fifth in the Townsend Thoresen Championship, and third in the Formula Ford Festival. Hill was offered some F3 drives and sponsorship for the following season, but these did not materialise. He then decided to take a leaf out of Niki Lauda's book and borrow a large loan (£100,000) in order to gain a drive. His first few years in F3 taught him a lot about car control and in 1988 he finished third in the British F3 championship and was rewarded with a test drive in a Benetton B187 F1 car. After two years of F3000, 1992 saw his break into Formula 1, driving the hopelessly outclassed Brabham, though he managed to qualify the car for the British Grand Prix. In 1993, Hill led at Silverstone, this time in a Williams, and he enjoyed an extremely successful season. During the following season he became team leader after the untimely death of Ayrton Senna. In his short career, Damon Hill has achieved a remarkable number of wins per grands prix raced, and become runner-up in the world championship twice in succession, the first time losing out by just one point as the victim of a controversial incident in the final race of the season.

## Grand Prix Wins

**1993**
Hungary
Belgium
Italy
**1994**
Spain
Britain
Belgium
Italy
Portugal
Japan
**1995**
Argentina
San Marino
Hungary
Australia

# 27

> "Whatever happens, life will stay the same afterwards. The sun will come up in the East and go down in the West. The World Championship is a good ambition. But I think there are a lot of important things to do in life. There are more things than just motor racing and world championships. I will not be too disappointed if I don't win. I will not be very happy if I fail, but I'm not going to get too excited about it."

## Carlos Reutemann

**Carlos Reutemann**, was born on 12 April 1942 at Santa Fe, Argentina, and was the first successful driver to emerge from that country since the retirement of the legendary Fangio. Reutemann learned to drive at the age of seven, driving his father's 1928 Model A Ford around the family's farm. He soon laid out a circuit on the farm and sharpened his skills there. After success in Argentinian races, where he was a triple touring car champion, Reutemann came to Europe in 1970 to drive in F2. He made headlines in his first race by taking out Jochen Rindt at the end of the first lap, yet recovered during the season finishing runner-up to Ronnie Peterson in the 1971 championship. In 1972, he drove for Bernie Ecclestone's Brabham team, and started his first ever Grand Prix in pole position in front of his home crowd. However, that season was ruined by a practice accident in an F2 race at Thruxton, resulting in a broken ankle and his Formula 1 boss banning him from racing at that level. Reutemann drove for Brabham for five years, winning four races with them before joining Ferrari and finishing third in the 1978 world championship. Reutemann's career was dogged by wrong decisions at vital times and he moved from Ferrari to join the previous year's champions at Lotus, only to see a Ferrari driver win the world title. After a disappointing year with Lotus, he joined the Williams team for 1980 as number two driver to Alan Jones, who went on to become champion. For that year, Reutemann was a good team-mate to Jones but the relationship soured when the thoughtful, yet moody, Argentinian decided to disobey team orders and stay ahead of Jones to win the 1981 Brazilian Grand Prix. His justification for his actions was that he was a racer and wouldn't give away a victory he had earned. That season should have seen Reutemann win the world title, but he let a big points lead disappear and although he started the final race in pole position and with a one-point lead, he let the race slip away from him and the title went to Piquet. Reutemann retired after that race, but when he heard that Jones had also retired he re-joined Williams only to finally give up after the second race of the 1982 season which saw team-mate Keke Rosberg become world champion. His popularity was still huge back in the Argentine, so much so that in 1991 he was elected Governor of Santa Fe province.

## Grand Prix Wins

**1974**
South Africa
Austria
USA
**1975**
Germany
**1977**
Brazil
**1978**
Brazil
USA - West
Britain
USA - East
**1980**
Monaco
**1981**
Brazil
Belgium

# 28

## Ronnie Peterson

> **"** Naturally I am fully aware of what I am doing and all the risks, but if you were going to think about them every time you got into the car, there'd never be any results. You know your limits and you try to keep within them, but on the other hand you must always try to push the limit a bit further. I don't do this just to become a millionaire, but in order to win and be the best in the world. **"**

## Grand Prix Wins

**1973**
France
Austria
Italy
USA
**1974**
Monaco
France
Italy
**1976**
Italy
**1978**
South Africa
Austria

*Bengt Ronald 'Ronnie' Peterson* was born on 14 February 1944 in Örebro, Sweden. He was the son of a baker and part-time engineer who raced 500cc bikes. Ronnie raced in moto-cross and speedway until his father built him a motor-cycle engined kart. He achieved a lot of success in karts before moving on to F3, winning at Monaco in 1969. His fast, "seat-of-the-pants" style soon got him noticed, and he started his first Grand Prix at Monaco. In 1971, a succession of second places earned him the runner-up spot in the world championship, and that same year he secured the European F2 Trophy series. In 1973 he joined Lotus to partner the new world champion, Emerson Fittipaldi. He immediately showed his astonishing speed and flair, but did not win a race until success arrived at Paul Ricard, a fast circuit. He re-joined March, his original F1 team, in 1976. A disastrous 1977 with the six-wheeled Tyrrell followed, where the man who was recognised as the fastest driver around, was slower than his team-mate, Patrick Depailler. He signed once more for Lotus in 1978, as number two driver to Mario Andretti. Although he was the faster of the two, Peterson realised the amount of work that Andretti had put into developing the Lotus. With total integrity, he would follow Andretti's car, only going on to win if the American had to stop. Andretti won the driver's title at Monza under the most tragic of circumstances. At the start of the race Peterson's car was pushed into the barriers. James Hunt was first on the scene and pulled him clear of the car. Although he had severe leg injuries, it was thought that Peterson would still survive. However, complications set in and he fell into a coma, dying on the morning of 11 September 1978.

## 29

## Gerhard Berger

> " I am a happy person and that's still my most important thing. Maybe you find people who say, 'The most important thing for me is to win everything,' but for me the most important thing is still my life. To win, it makes me happy but some other things make me happy so I follow all the things that make me happy. "

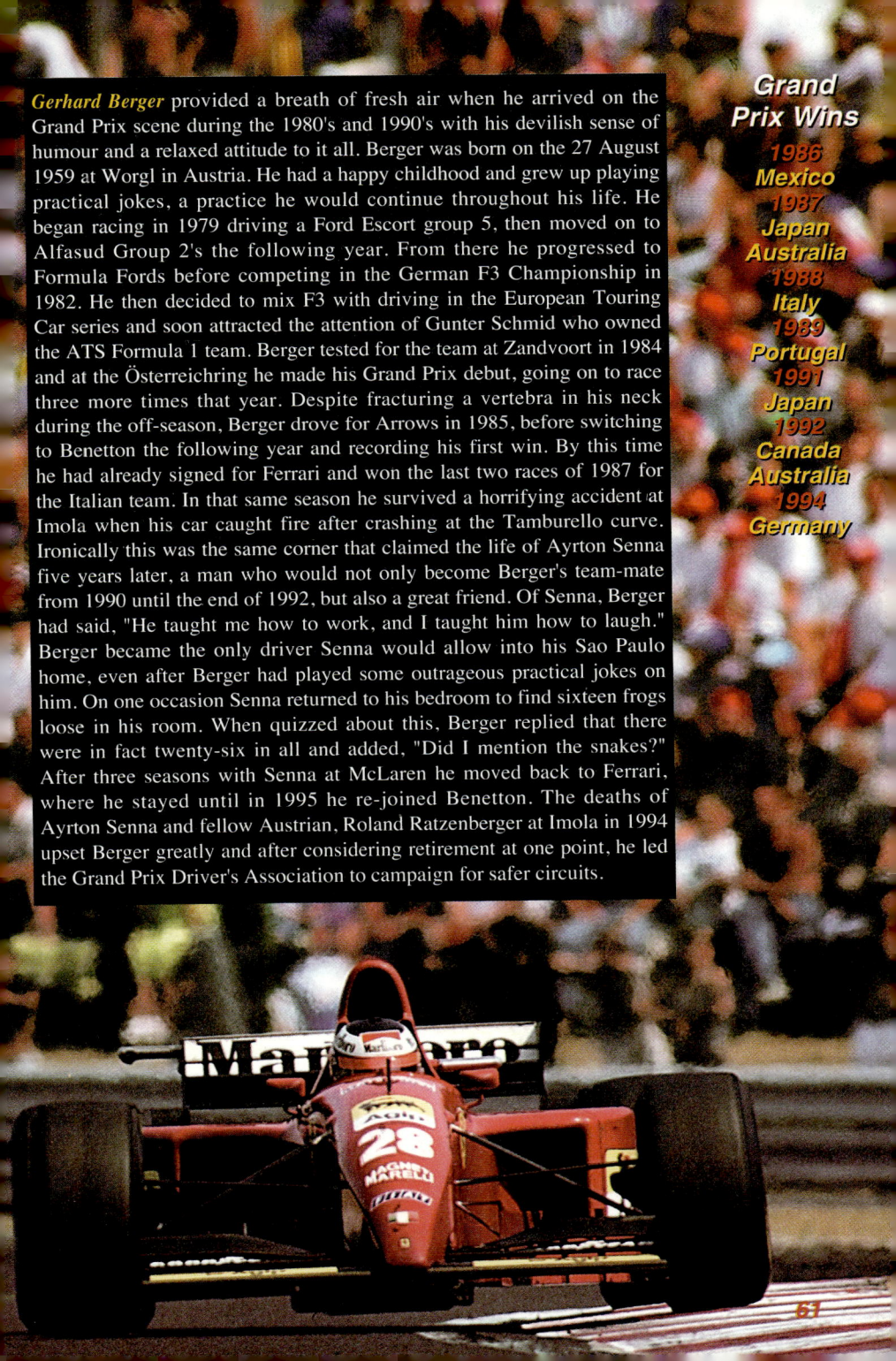

*Gerhard Berger* provided a breath of fresh air when he arrived on the Grand Prix scene during the 1980's and 1990's with his devilish sense of humour and a relaxed attitude to it all. Berger was born on the 27 August 1959 at Worgl in Austria. He had a happy childhood and grew up playing practical jokes, a practice he would continue throughout his life. He began racing in 1979 driving a Ford Escort group 5, then moved on to Alfasud Group 2's the following year. From there he progressed to Formula Fords before competing in the German F3 Championship in 1982. He then decided to mix F3 with driving in the European Touring Car series and soon attracted the attention of Gunter Schmid who owned the ATS Formula 1 team. Berger tested for the team at Zandvoort in 1984 and at the Österreichring he made his Grand Prix debut, going on to race three more times that year. Despite fracturing a vertebra in his neck during the off-season, Berger drove for Arrows in 1985, before switching to Benetton the following year and recording his first win. By this time he had already signed for Ferrari and won the last two races of 1987 for the Italian team. In that same season he survived a horrifying accident at Imola when his car caught fire after crashing at the Tamburello curve. Ironically this was the same corner that claimed the life of Ayrton Senna five years later, a man who would not only become Berger's team-mate from 1990 until the end of 1992, but also a great friend. Of Senna, Berger had said, "He taught me how to work, and I taught him how to laugh." Berger became the only driver Senna would allow into his Sao Paulo home, even after Berger had played some outrageous practical jokes on him. On one occasion Senna returned to his bedroom to find sixteen frogs loose in his room. When quizzed about this, Berger replied that there were in fact twenty-six in all and added, "Did I mention the snakes?" After three seasons with Senna at McLaren he moved back to Ferrari, where he stayed until in 1995 he re-joined Benetton. The deaths of Ayrton Senna and fellow Austrian, Roland Ratzenberger at Imola in 1994 upset Berger greatly and after considering retirement at one point, he led the Grand Prix Driver's Association to campaign for safer circuits.

## Grand Prix Wins

*1986*
**Mexico**
*1987*
**Japan**
**Australia**
*1988*
**Italy**
*1989*
**Portugal**
*1991*
**Japan**
*1992*
**Canada**
**Australia**
*1994*
**Germany**

# 30

## Jacky Ickx

" *Motor racing has given me everything, a great bundle of happiness of all sorts. I am the last person in the world to complain about my career. What is certain is that I have always driven for the pleasure of driving.* "

*Jacques Bernard Ickx* was born in Brussels on 1 January 1945, the son of a motor racing journalist. He learnt to ride a motor cycle and showed a natural flair for racing them. His first experience of car racing came in hill-climbs, then after completing his National Service, Ickx returned to drive sports cars which would prove to be his most successful form of racing, winning Le Mans a record six times. After several races for Ken Tyrrell in F3 and F2, he announced his arrival in the 1967 German Grand Prix when his F2 Matra qualified third fastest and this fine performance led to a drive for Ferrari in 1968. He challenged for the World Championship up until the Canadian Grand Prix when he broke his leg. In 1969 Ickx switched to Brabham, a move orchestrated by Gulf Oil who wanted Ickx to drive in their GT40 sports cars. The following year Ickx re-joined Ferrari and finished runner-up in the championship. After a further two years at Ferrari he joined Team Lotus, before moving to Wolf-Williams at the start of the 1976 season, only to move once again, this time to Ensign for the tail-end of the year. Ickx's final stint in Grand Prix racing came in 1979 when he deputised for Patrick Depailler in the Ligier, following the Frenchman's hang-gliding accident. He continued with his highly successful sports car career, but his involvement with Formula One did not stop as he was made Clerk of the Course at Monaco. His licence was withdrawn after the controversial stoppage of the 1984 race while Alain Prost led. Ickx was later exonerated from favouring Prost, leaving his great Le Mans record as the lasting testament to his talent.

## Grand Prix Wins

*1968*
France
*1969*
Germany
Canada
*1970*
Austria
Canada
Mexico
*1971*
Holland
*1972*
Germany

## 31

### René Arnoux

> "The duel with Gilles (Villeneuve at Dijon in 1979) is something I'll never forget, my greatest souvenir of racing. You can only race like that, you know, with someone you trust completely, and you don't meet many people like him. He beat me, yes, and in France, but it didn't worry me - I knew I'd been beaten by the best driver in the world."

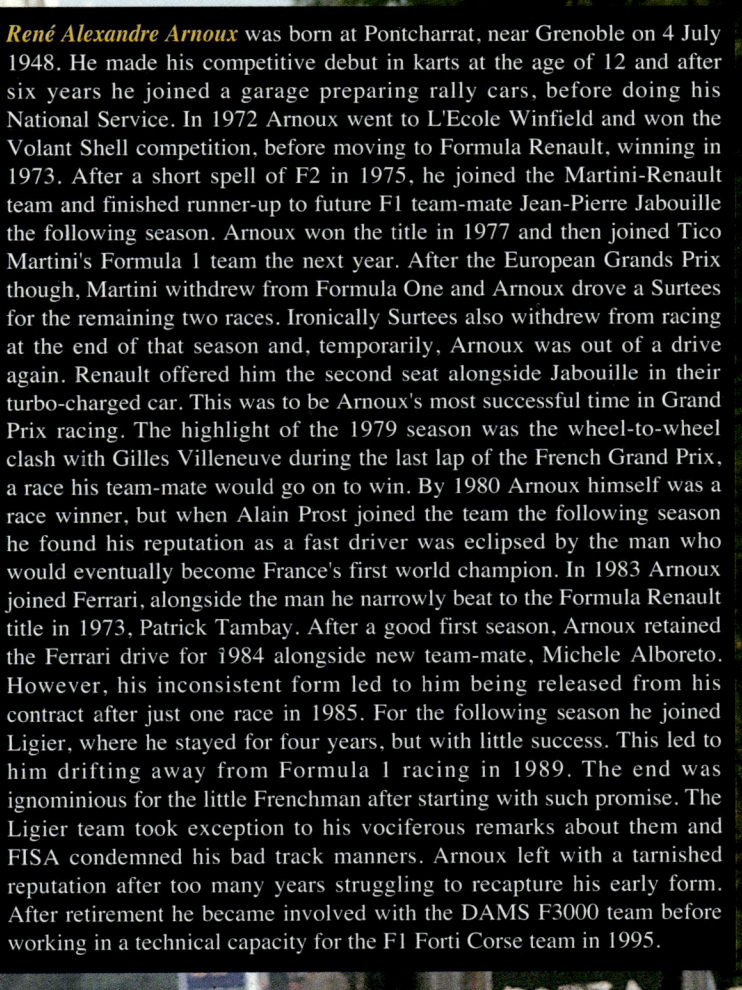

*René Alexandre Arnoux* was born at Pontcharrat, near Grenoble on 4 July 1948. He made his competitive debut in karts at the age of 12 and after six years he joined a garage preparing rally cars, before doing his National Service. In 1972 Arnoux went to L'Ecole Winfield and won the Volant Shell competition, before moving to Formula Renault, winning in 1973. After a short spell of F2 in 1975, he joined the Martini-Renault team and finished runner-up to future F1 team-mate Jean-Pierre Jabouille the following season. Arnoux won the title in 1977 and then joined Tico Martini's Formula 1 team the next year. After the European Grands Prix though, Martini withdrew from Formula One and Arnoux drove a Surtees for the remaining two races. Ironically Surtees also withdrew from racing at the end of that season and, temporarily, Arnoux was out of a drive again. Renault offered him the second seat alongside Jabouille in their turbo-charged car. This was to be Arnoux's most successful time in Grand Prix racing. The highlight of the 1979 season was the wheel-to-wheel clash with Gilles Villeneuve during the last lap of the French Grand Prix, a race his team-mate would go on to win. By 1980 Arnoux himself was a race winner, but when Alain Prost joined the team the following season he found his reputation as a fast driver was eclipsed by the man who would eventually become France's first world champion. In 1983 Arnoux joined Ferrari, alongside the man he narrowly beat to the Formula Renault title in 1973, Patrick Tambay. After a good first season, Arnoux retained the Ferrari drive for 1984 alongside new team-mate, Michele Alboreto. However, his inconsistent form led to him being released from his contract after just one race in 1985. For the following season he joined Ligier, where he stayed for four years, but with little success. This led to him drifting away from Formula 1 racing in 1989. The end was ignominious for the little Frenchman after starting with such promise. The Ligier team took exception to his vociferous remarks about them and FISA condemned his bad track manners. Arnoux left with a tarnished reputation after too many years struggling to recapture his early form. After retirement he became involved with the DAMS F3000 team before working in a technical capacity for the F1 Forti Corse team in 1995.

## Grand Prix Wins

*1980*
Brazil
South Africa
*1982*
France
Italy
*1983*
Canada
Germany
Holland

# 32
## Riccardo Patrese

> "Because drivers like to play politics, they have problems staying together in the same team. I am not saying I am the nice guy, but I play my cards on the table. Maybe I will not be remembered as a world champion, but I would like to be remembered as a person who always said what he thought and never played funny games with anybody."

*Riccardo Patrese* became one of the most popular men in the pit lane after being labelled 'the most dangerous driver in Formula One' during his first years in Grand Prix racing. Born on 17 April 1954 in Padua, Italy, the young Patrese displayed early signs of his sporting prowess when he became Italian Junior swimming champion and reaching national standard in ski-ing. However, it was in motor racing where he would make his mark, and he worked his way through the ranks until he made his Grand Prix debut with Shadow in 1977 at Monaco. The following season he joined Arrows and led the South African Grand Prix until he retired with engine problems. It was at Monza that he hit the headlines, being blamed for causing the accident that cost Ronnie Peterson his life. Patrese had got himself the reputation of being an aggressive and dangerous driver, but away from the circuit he was always a quiet, shy man. Eventually he was absolved of responsibility for Peterson's death, but it took a while to shake off the label that some people had given him. He moved from Arrows in 1982 to join Brabham as number two driver to Nelson Piquet. Luck played its part in his first Grand Prix win when he emerged the winner of a race he thought he had lost after spinning and losing the lead, only for subsequent leaders to retire. He won his second Grand Prix a year later, then had to wait a long time for his next success, trying a move to Alfa Romeo in 1984 before returning to Brabham. In 1988 he joined Nigel Mansell at Williams, ending his drought in 1990 by winning at Imola. His relaxed and easy nature made him an ideal team-mate and he became not only a popular driver, but by 1989 he had started in more Grands Prix than any other driver in history. After the 1993 season, by which time he had joined Benetton, he had started in 256 Grands Prix, scoring 281 points. He was without a drive for 1994 and 1995, so he switched his attention to touring cars and competed in the German DTM series.

## Grand Prix Wins

**1982**
Monaco
**1983**
South Africa
**1990**
San Marino
**1991**
Mexico
Portugal
**1992**
Japan

**33**

**Gilles Villeneuve**

> "I don't have any fear of a crash. I never think I can hurt myself. It seems impossible to me. If you believe it can happen to you, how can you possibly do the job properly? If you're never over eight-tenths, because you're thinking about a shunt, you're not going as quick as you can. And if you're not doing that, you're not a racing driver."

*Gilles Villeneuve* was born in Berthierville, Quebec on 18 January 1950. The French-Canadian was introduced to high-speed sport at the age of eight when he started to race snowmobiles, winning the Canadian championship in 1973 and the world title three years later. His first win paid for a Formula Ford car, in which he won 70% of his races. He then moved on to Canadian Formula Atlantic and in 1976 he beat many top F1 drivers - including Britain's James Hunt - in the Trois Rivières race at Mosport. When Hunt returned to England after the race, he raved about Villeneuve to his McLaren boss, Teddy Mayer. Villeneuve was given his Grand Prix debut the following year in Britain and was so impressive he was awarded the 'Man of the Meeting' prize. McLaren did not race Villeneuve again and Ferrari leapt at the chance of securing the services of the man Enzo Ferrari saw as the new Nuvolari. His Ferrari debut came at his home Grand Prix, where he was classified twelfth, after retiring four laps from the end with a broken driveshaft. Villeneuve was retained by Ferrari for the next year, and raced for them for the rest of his tragically short career. Villeneuve's all-out style won over the hearts of the Italian 'tifosi'. His car control was legendary and in his hands the Ferrari would be flung around a circuit in a way no other driver could match. After finishing runner-up to team-mate Jody Scheckter in 1979, the Ferraris were outclassed the following year, but the introduction of turbo-charged engines in 1981 saw the resurgence of the prancing horse. Although the car was not in the same class as the opposition, Villeneuve took it to two brilliant wins and the legend of 'number 27' was born. Season 1982 promised much, but there was a bitter falling out with team-mate Pironi at Imola when Villeneuve should have won and Pironi disobeyed team orders. The next race saw the death of the little French-Canadian during practice and the world lost a truly great driver.

## Grand Prix Wins

**1978**
Canada
**1979**
South Africa
USA - West
USA - East
**1981**
Monaco
Spain

# 34

## Jacques Laffite

> "What I enjoy is developing the car, driving a more and more competitive car, and then trying to win with it. It's quite simple. I derive satisfaction from starting in ninth place on the grid and finishing second or third, or even winning."

*Jacques-Henri Laffite*, the son of a leading Paris lawyer, was born on 21 November 1943, in Magny-Cours, France. As a schoolboy he took an interest in motor racing, and when he left school he became a mechanic looking after Jean-Pierre Jabouille's F3 car, then worked for the Winfield Racing School. Laffite drove in F3 himself in 1969, yet found the cost restricting and stepped down to Formula Renault, winning the title in 1972. With that success he went back into F3 and won the French championship in 1973, including the important Monaco Grand Prix support race. In 1974 he drove in F2, finishing third in the European championship, and made his Grand Prix debut in a Williams Iso car in Germany. He continued with Frank Williams' team the following year, finishing second at the Nürburgring and bringing much needed revenue to the team. He also won the F2 European championship, and became Group Six sports car world champion. This drew the attention of the French Ligier team and he was signed to drive for them in 1976 which signalled the start of a very successful partnership. He secured some fine results in his first season with the team, finishing second in Austria and third at Monza. The next year saw the first-ever all-French championship Grand Prix win at Anderstorp and was the first of his six wins for Ligier. In 1979 Laffite - and Ligier - enjoyed their most successful season as the Ligier JS11 dominated the first two races, then fought with Ferrari for wins over the first half of the season. Laffite finished fourth by the end of the year, a feat he would repeat in 1981 when he went to the final Grand Prix of the year with an outside chance of the championship, yet Piquet and the two Williams' drivers finished ahead of him. He moved to Williams in 1983 and developed his love of golf as well as that of racing. The genial Frenchman fitted in very well with the team, but was replaced by Mansell in 1985, so he rejoined Ligier and would have beaten Graham Hill's then record of Grand Prix starts were it not for an accident at the beginning of the 1986 British Grand Prix which resulted in two broken legs and the end of his F1 career. Laffite recovered enough to drive saloon cars, and in the mid-nineties he re-joined the F1 ranks as a consultant for Ligier.

## Grand Prix Wins

*1977*
**Sweden**
*1979*
**Argentina**
**Brazil**
*1980*
**Germany**
*1981*
**Austria**
**Canada**

## 35

## Tony Brooks

> "I always felt it was morally wrong to take unnecessary risks with one's life because I believe that life is a gift from God, and that suicide is morally unacceptable. I suppose there are those who would say that driving racing cars at all is an unnecessary risk, but I wouldn't agree with that."

**Charles Anthony Standish (Tony) Brooks** was destined to become a dentist until a friend lent him a Healey Silverstone car to drive in club races, where he had his fair share of victories. Born in Dunkinfield, Cheshire on 25 February 1932, Tony Brooks received a great compliment from Fangio. When the Argentinian was asked who would succeed him as world champion after his retirement, Fangio named Brooks. Sadly this was not to be fulfilled, yet Brooks starred in some great performances, notably in 1958 when he won at Spa, Nürburgring and Monza. Brooks's career really took off in 1955, when he was offered a drive in an F1 Connaught at the Syracuse Grand Prix in Sicily. This was a daunting task as Brooks had never raced abroad, nor even raced an F1 car before. However, no-one would have suspected this as he qualified third, then went on to win handsomely, beating many of the world championship contenders who had turned up to compete in this non-championship race. In winning the race, he not only set a new lap record, but became the first British driver in a British car to win on the continent for thirty-one years. For the 1956 season BRM signed Brooks to partner Mike Hawthorn, but success eluded him and he joined Vanwall the following year. He made a valuable contribution to the team, not least when he let team-leader Stirling Moss take over his car in order to win the British Grand Prix, revealing the obliging and generous temperament of Brooks. In 1959 Brooks joined Ferrari and added to his tally of Grands Prix victories, although the Cooper of Jack Brabham dominated the year, leaving Brooks as runner-up in the championship. By this time Brooks was thinking about retirement and he established a garage business in Byfleet near the Brooklands race track, prompting a move back to England and joining an English team. No more Grands Prix successes came his way and he finally retired in 1961. He was a very popular man in the sport and his good manners and consideration for others earned him wide respect. After retirement he concentrated on his garage business, which later became a successful Ford dealership.

## Grand Prix Wins

**1957**
Britain
(shared with Stirling Moss)
**1958**
Belgium
Germany
Italy
**1959**
France
Germany

# 36

## Clay Regazzoni

> "You must understand that, for me, it's not a matter of winning all the time. I am quite happy just to be a part of Formula One – I love it, and most of all I love to drive racing cars. So why should I stop when I feel this way?"

*Gianclaudio Giuseppe 'Clay' Regazzoni* was born in Lugano, an Italian-speaking part of Switzerland, on 5 September 1939. He was the son of a coachbuilder, and joined his father's business at the age of eighteen. He became interested in motor racing, competing in hillclimbs in 1963 before qualifying for a racing licence at the Montlhéry racing course in France. His progress through F3 and F2 was characterised by speed and accidents. In 1968 he was involved in a controversial accident when he collided with Chris Lambert's Brabham and the Englishman was killed. However, Regazzoni was exonerated and by 1970 he was a member of the Ferrari F1 team, having raced F2 for them the previous season. He finished fourth in his first Grand Prix in Holland. The season was to end in tragedy with the death of Jochen Rindt at Monza, a race which Regazzoni went on to win in magnificent fashion to the delight of the Ferrari-loving crowd. Regazzoni finished third in the world championship following a consistent run of results at the end of the season. He stayed with the Italian team until 1973 when Enzo Ferrari threatened to quit motor racing and release his drivers from their contracts. It was a threat which he never carried out, but which forced Regazzoni to join BRM. It was an uncompetitive year and nearly a costly one when Regazzoni's car caught fire in the South African Grand Prix, Mike Hailwood dragging the unconscious Swiss driver out of his cockpit. In 1974, Regazzoni returned to Ferrari where he partnered new star Niki Lauda and finished runner-up in the world championship, only three points behind champion Emerson Fittipaldi. In 1977 he was replaced by Carlos Reutemann, yet his enthusiasm and love of competition meant he was quite happy to be in smaller teams' cars, driving for Ensign and Shadow in consecutive seasons. His luck changed in 1979 when he joined Frank Williams' team to drive the remarkable FW07, finishing second in Monaco, winning the British Grand Prix and completing a Williams one-two behind Alan Jones in Germany. Regazzoni surprised everyone by moving back to Ensign the following season, but it was a decision which was to have tragic consequences. In the Long Beach Grand Prix his car lost its brakes and he broke both his legs and crushed a vertebra. He was confined to a wheelchair from then on, and although he could stand, he could no longer walk. He remained involved with F1 by commentating for Swiss television.

## Grand Prix Wins

*1970*
**Italy**
*1974*
**Germany**
*1975*
**Italy**
*1976*
**USA - West**
*1979*
**Britain**

# 37

> "It's a violent sport, and not just because of the danger, but because of the power of the machinery involved. I get satisfaction out of taming that power and making it look unviolent."

## John Watson

*John Watson,* born in Belfast on 4 May 1946, was born into a racing family. His father, Marshall, had won the first ever saloon car race in Ireland, and after watching his father, John decided that motor racing was for him. He joined the family garage business after leaving school and it provided the funds to help the young Watson progress through the ranks up to F2. He competed in F2 for three years from 1969 before Bernie Ecclestone signed him to drive for Brabham in F2 with occasional F1 races. In 1973 he made his Grand Prix debut at Silverstone and earned his first world championship point at Monaco a year later. In 1975 he drove for Team Surtees before taking over Mark Donohue's seat at Penske following the American's fatal accident in Austria. Good performances saw him earn a contract for 1976 in a car that was very competitive. By the time the Austrian Grand Prix came around, he had been fourth in South Africa and third in both France and Britain. Watson then triumphed in Austria and he was then forced to shave off his beard as a result of a deal with Roger Penske, who disliked hirsute drivers. Watson was re-signed by Brabham in 1977, becoming team leader following the death of Carlos Pace in a flying accident. Bad luck dogged his season, and he missed out on his second Grand Prix victory in France when he slowed down with fuel problems, which let Mario Andretti through to win on the final lap. He stayed with Brabham to partner Niki Lauda in 1978, securing a second and two third places before joining McLaren. In 1981 he won the British Grand Prix amid great jubilation, then found himself within reach of the championship near the end of the following season after two more Grand Prix successes, only to be replaced in 1984 by Alain Prost. Watson made his final appearance in the 1985 European Grand Prix, but by then he was establishing a reputation in Group C Jaguars. He retired from competitive racing and set up the John Watson Performance Driving Centre at Silverstone, though he remained involved with F1 as a commentator for Eurosport.

## Grand Prix Wins

**1976**
*Austria*
**1981**
*Britain*
**1982**
*Belgium*
*USA - East*
**1983**
*USA - West*

**38**

"*Just racing for the money is not enough; you must really work hard to win.*"

## Michele Alboreto

*Michele Alboreto* - born in Milan on 23 December 1956 - harboured dreams of becoming a racing driver from a very early age. He was the son of a hard working and financially secure Lombard family basing values on hard work and building on success. By the time he got to technical college he was a good student, but not averse to taking time off to visit Monza. Once his parents realised he was determined to follow a racing path, their encouragement helped Alboreto enormously. His father bought him a motor bike, which he promptly sold for a half share in a Formula Monza car. However, the friend he bought it with did not pass his driving test, so he needed a new partner. Simone Vullo then came onto the scene and said if Alboreto was faster than him he could keep the car - which he did. In 1978 Alboreto was working as a clerk in a children's wear company, but soon a racing career took over as he progressed through F2 and F3. He made his debut in a Tyrrell at Imola in 1981 and in the following year he won the Las Vegas Grand Prix. Two years later, he won in Detroit, which proved to be the last non-turbo win until 1989. For 1984 Alboreto became the first Italian to win in a Ferrari since Ludovico Scarfiotti at the 1966 Italian Grand Prix. Alboreto's fortunes improved in 1985, leading the drivers' championship for most of the summer until Prost beat him to the world title at Brands Hatch in October. He remained at Ferrari for three more years, but did not add to his list of victories and in 1989 he returned briefly to Tyrrell for six races before moving to the Larrousse Lola team for the rest of the season. In 1990 he joined the Footwork Arrows team and would remain with them for the next three years, before driving for Minardi in 1994, where he picked up a solitary point in Monaco. For 1995 he took up German Touring Cars as no F1 drives were on offer to him, despite 194 Grands Prix, and 186½ points.

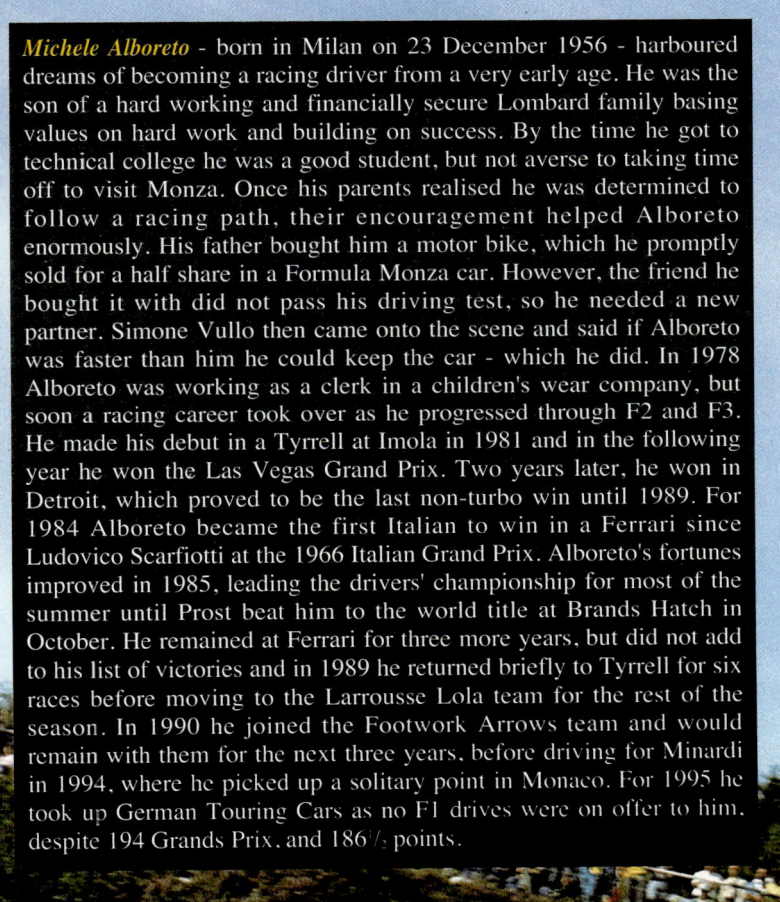

## Grand Prix Wins

**1982**
Las Vegas
**1983**
USA - East
**1984**
Belgium
**1985**
Canada
Germany

# 39

"There is no perfect race. It's a fact, so it doesn't do any good to stew over it."

## Dan Gurney

*Daniel Sexton Gurney* was born in Port Jefferson, New York on 13 April 1931. When his opera singer father retired, the family moved to California which meant that by 1950 Dan was able to join the racers on the Bonneville salt flats. Indeed, his love of speed meant that he was often in trouble with the local police for staging impromptu drag races on the streets. His motor racing exploits were interrupted whilst he served in the US Army in Korea during 1952, but on his return his success in sports cars led to a works Ferrari test and a drive alongside Phil Hill and Tony Brooks in 1960. Because the pay was poor for Ferrari drivers, Gurney made a move to BRM but the only saving grace that season was a win in the Nürburgring 1000km sports car race. In 1961 he joined Porsche, and although the Ferraris dominated, Gurney finished in joint third place in the championship. The following year he won his first Grand Prix, but after Porsche withdrew from racing at the end of the year, Gurney joined Jack Brabham's team. Although he raced well he was often let down by mechanical problems. With the change to the new 3-litre F1 regulations in 1966, Gurney decided to start his own team and established All American Racers in California to enter cars at Indianapolis and in the world championship. His new cars were called Eagles and Gurney won the 1967 Race of Champions and Belgian Grand Prix. However, the strain of running a world championship team, an Indianapolis racer and a failing marriage all took their toll on Gurney. The Eagle Grand Prix project ended in 1968 along with Gurney's enthusiasm for racing following the death of Jim Clark. Gurney replaced Bruce McLaren after the New Zealander died in 1970, but his appetite for racing had gone, though Eagle Indy cars continued until 1983. Gurney continued to involve himself in the sport through running Toyota's IMSA racing programme.

## Grand Prix Wins

**1962**
France
**1964**
France, Mexico
**1967**
Belgium

**40**

**Bruce McLaren**

> " To do something well is so worthwhile that to die trying to do it better cannot be foolhardy. Life is measured in achievement, not in years alone. "

*Bruce McLaren* was born on 30 August 1937 in Remvera, New Zealand, the son of a garage owner. At a young age he wanted to pursue a motor cycling career, but these hopes were dashed when, at the age of nine, he contracted Perthes disease, a hip illness. Two years later he could walk again, but the disease had left him with a permanent limp and over-developed shoulder and arm muscles due to his reliance on wheelchairs and crutches. For his sixteenth birthday, his father gave him an Austin 7 and his motor sport career began. He studied engineering and pursued his racing at the same time. These two skills would prove to be huge assets as he became one of the two most successful exponents of the driver-turned-constructor group of men. After six years of engineering studies and driving, he came to England through the 'Driver to Europe' scheme. He transported his F2 Cooper over to join him in 1958 and his performances won him a seat in the factory Cooper team for 1959. His team-mate, Jack Brabham, clinched the title at the end of the year after McLaren had secured his first grand prix win. During the following year he played a very supportive role again to Brabham, finishing runner-up. Brabham then went on to form his own team, leaving McLaren as team leader at Cooper. In 1964, McLaren followed Brabham's lead and set up Bruce McLaren Motor Racing, winning the Tasman championship, but losing team-mate Tim Mayer in practice for the final race. He quit Cooper at the end of 1965 to concentrate on building and racing his own range of cars. The foundations of McLaren's team were laid when Mayer's brother, Teddy, took over the business side and remained in charge until 1981. Meanwhile, McLaren went on to win the 1968 Belgian Grand Prix in a car bearing his name, again emulating Jack Brabham. More success was to be found in Can-Am racing where McLaren cars dominated, and McLaren won the championship in 1967 and 1969, with Denny Hulme winning in between. However, whilst testing the car for the 1970 series McLaren lost his life. On 2 June he went on a flying lap around the Goodwood circuit when his car left the main straight and crashed. The world of motor racing had lost one of its brightest stars, though the name of McLaren was destined to live on.

## Grand Prix Wins

**1959**
USA
**1960**
Argentina
**1962**
Monaco
**1968**
Belgium

# 41

## Peter Collins

> "I'm only twenty-five years old and have plenty of time to win the championship on my own."

**Grand Prix Wins**

**1956**
Belgium
France

**1958**
Britain

*Peter Collins* - the son of a successful motor trader in Kidderminster - was born on 8 November 1931 in Mustow Green. He began his career in a Cooper-Norton 500 at the age of seventeen. He spent three years in Formula 500 before he joined the HWM F2 team alongside Stirling Moss and Lance Macklin in 1951. He was signed for Ferrari in 1956, and had a marvellous first season with the Italian team. After two victories he was challenging for the world championship. At Monza, in what could have been his finest hour, he selflessly gave his car to Fangio to complete the race and become the world champion again. This action meant that he would always be revered in Italy for helping a Ferrari driver become champion. It had been said that Collins himself could have been world champion that day, but he believed that he had plenty of time in which to achieve that. He enjoyed life to the full and became firm friends with Mike Hawthorn, another dashing young Englishman, and they became known as the 'Mon-Ami Mates'. In 1957 Collins married an American, Louise King, and they soon became the golden couple living an extravagant lifestyle based on a yacht moored in the harbour at Monaco. Tales of Collins and Hawthorn became legendary, and one reported incident was at the start of Le Mans in 1958 when the friends were to share a Ferrari. Hawthorn was still chatting to a pretty girl as the other drivers were lining up for their sprint to the cars. As time ticked by Collins shouted to Hawthorn, "Come on, Mike, blow the car up quickly and let's get back to the boat!" Later that year Collins won the British Grand Prix at Silverstone in glorious fashion, with Hawthorn coming second. The next race of the season, however, ended in tragedy. On lap ten of the German Grand Prix on 3 August, Collins lost control on the right hand turn at Pflanzgarten in full view of Hawthorn, who drove on before retiring one lap later. Despite being flown by helicopter to a Bonn hospital, Collins died from the head injuries sustained in the crash.

## 42

### Didier Pironi

> "The only thing that interests me in Formula One is the World Championship. If, for any reason, I began to think that I couldn't win it I would stop racing. I don't want to spend my life in Formula One for the sake of it."

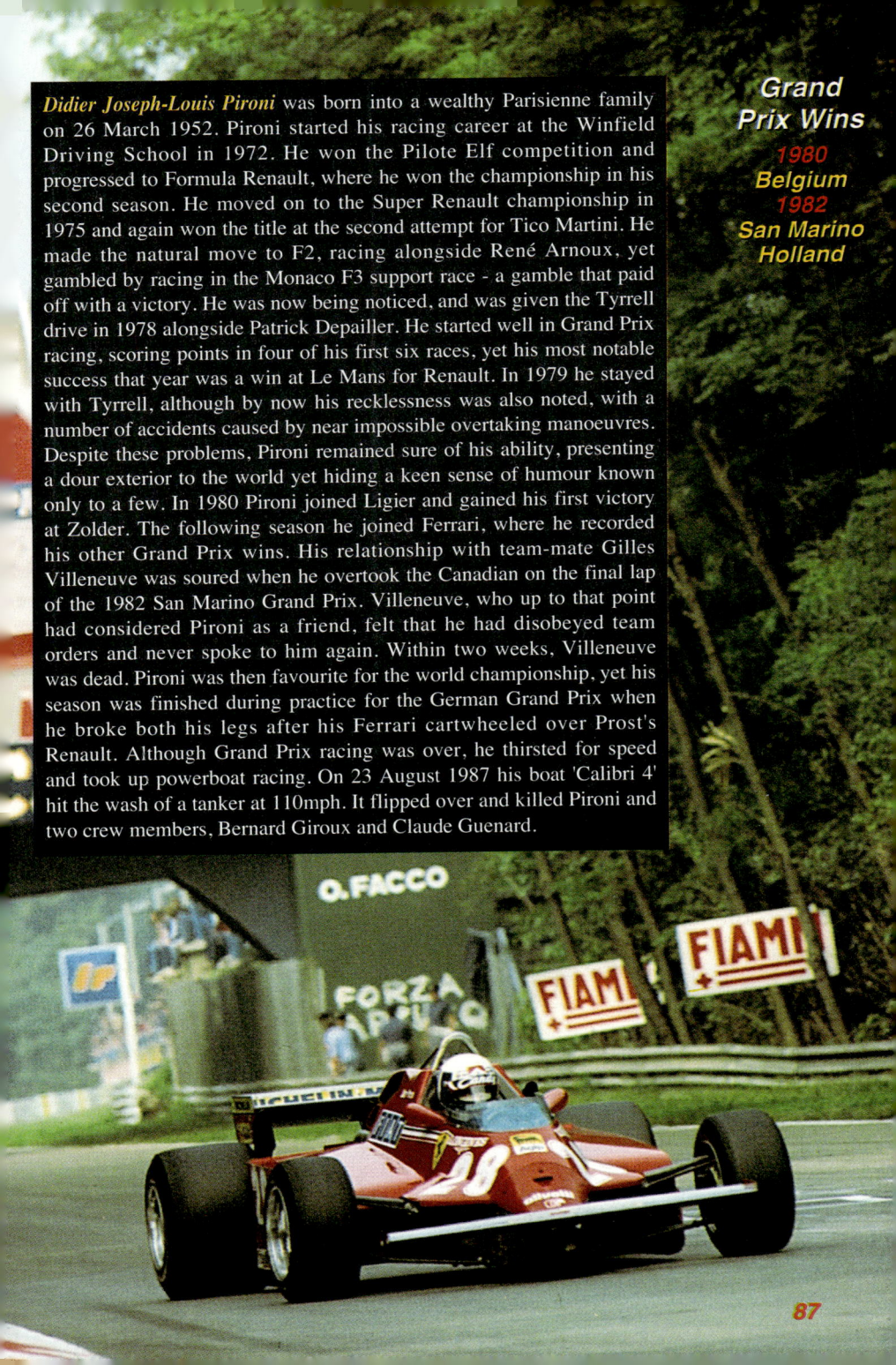

**Didier Joseph-Louis Pironi** was born into a wealthy Parisienne family on 26 March 1952. Pironi started his racing career at the Winfield Driving School in 1972. He won the Pilote Elf competition and progressed to Formula Renault, where he won the championship in his second season. He moved on to the Super Renault championship in 1975 and again won the title at the second attempt for Tico Martini. He made the natural move to F2, racing alongside René Arnoux, yet gambled by racing in the Monaco F3 support race - a gamble that paid off with a victory. He was now being noticed, and was given the Tyrrell drive in 1978 alongside Patrick Depailler. He started well in Grand Prix racing, scoring points in four of his first six races, yet his most notable success that year was a win at Le Mans for Renault. In 1979 he stayed with Tyrrell, although by now his recklessness was also noted, with a number of accidents caused by near impossible overtaking manoeuvres. Despite these problems, Pironi remained sure of his ability, presenting a dour exterior to the world yet hiding a keen sense of humour known only to a few. In 1980 Pironi joined Ligier and gained his first victory at Zolder. The following season he joined Ferrari, where he recorded his other Grand Prix wins. His relationship with team-mate Gilles Villeneuve was soured when he overtook the Canadian on the final lap of the 1982 San Marino Grand Prix. Villeneuve, who up to that point had considered Pironi as a friend, felt that he had disobeyed team orders and never spoke to him again. Within two weeks, Villeneuve was dead. Pironi was then favourite for the world championship, yet his season was finished during practice for the German Grand Prix when he broke both his legs after his Ferrari cartwheeled over Prost's Renault. Although Grand Prix racing was over, he thirsted for speed and took up powerboat racing. On 23 August 1987 his boat 'Calibri 4' hit the wash of a tanker at 110mph. It flipped over and killed Pironi and two crew members, Bernard Giroux and Claude Guenard.

### Grand Prix Wins

*1980*
Belgium
*1982*
San Marino
Holland

**43**

**Thierry Boutsen**

> " Whatever I do, I prefer to be slow to start with and learn what the car and the circuit is all about. I don't see the merit in being instantly quick and risking throwing it all away with a silly mistake later on which could have been avoided by spending a little longer finding out how it all works. "

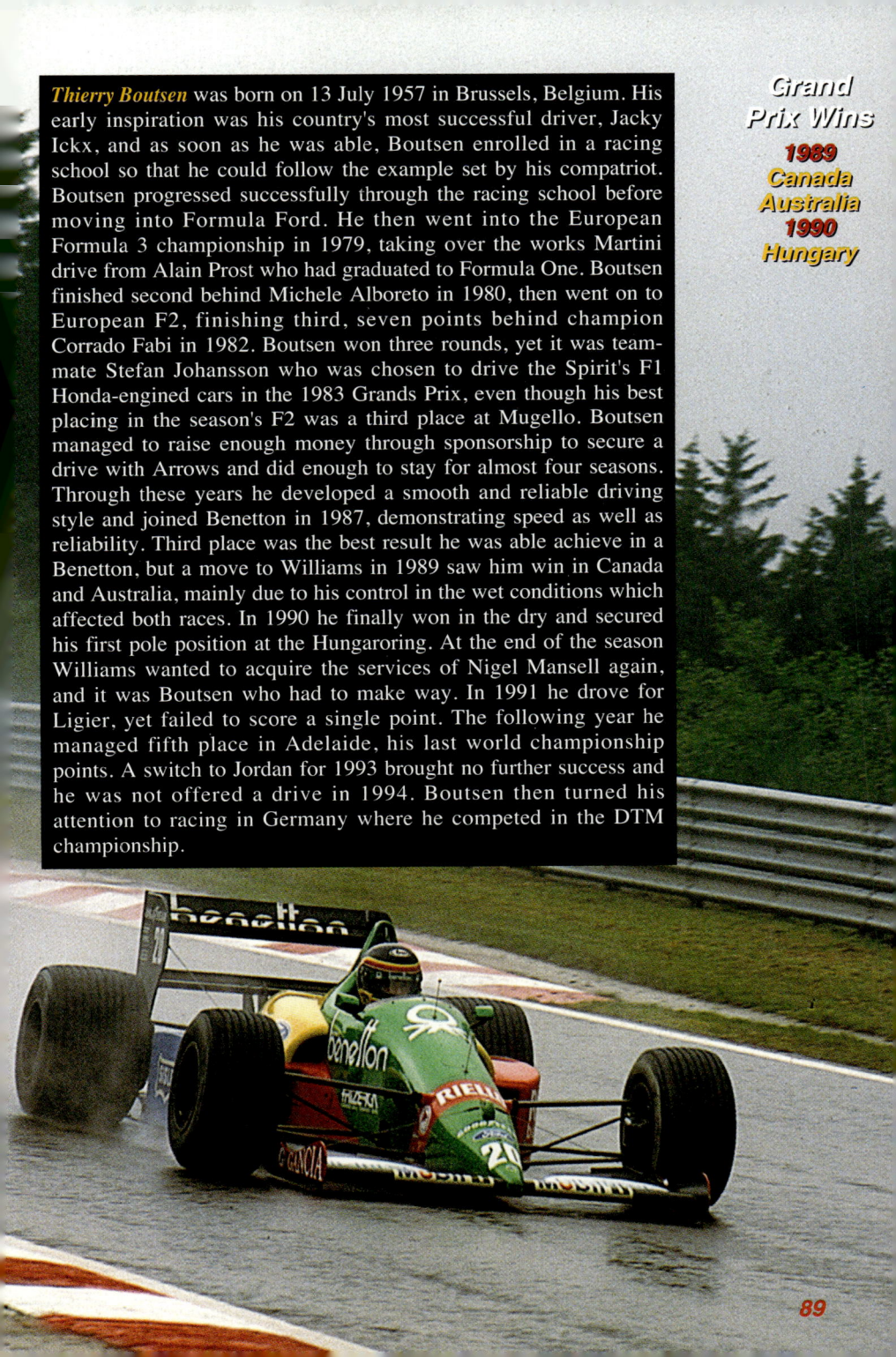

***Thierry Boutsen*** was born on 13 July 1957 in Brussels, Belgium. His early inspiration was his country's most successful driver, Jacky Ickx, and as soon as he was able, Boutsen enrolled in a racing school so that he could follow the example set by his compatriot. Boutsen progressed successfully through the racing school before moving into Formula Ford. He then went into the European Formula 3 championship in 1979, taking over the works Martini drive from Alain Prost who had graduated to Formula One. Boutsen finished second behind Michele Alboreto in 1980, then went on to European F2, finishing third, seven points behind champion Corrado Fabi in 1982. Boutsen won three rounds, yet it was teammate Stefan Johansson who was chosen to drive the Spirit's F1 Honda-engined cars in the 1983 Grands Prix, even though his best placing in the season's F2 was a third place at Mugello. Boutsen managed to raise enough money through sponsorship to secure a drive with Arrows and did enough to stay for almost four seasons. Through these years he developed a smooth and reliable driving style and joined Benetton in 1987, demonstrating speed as well as reliability. Third place was the best result he was able achieve in a Benetton, but a move to Williams in 1989 saw him win in Canada and Australia, mainly due to his control in the wet conditions which affected both races. In 1990 he finally won in the dry and secured his first pole position at the Hungaroring. At the end of the season Williams wanted to acquire the services of Nigel Mansell again, and it was Boutsen who had to make way. In 1991 he drove for Ligier, yet failed to score a single point. The following year he managed fifth place in Adelaide, his last world championship points. A switch to Jordan for 1993 brought no further success and he was not offered a drive in 1994. Boutsen then turned his attention to racing in Germany where he competed in the DTM championship.

**Grand Prix Wins**
*1989*
Canada
Australia
*1990*
Hungary

# 44

## Froilan Gonzalez

> On the winner's podium (at Silverstone in 1951) I was embraced warmly by Fangio. That meant a lot to me. Then they played the Argentine national anthem. I had never experienced anything like this before. When I saw my country's flag being hoisted, it was just too much for me and I cried. That moment will live with me for ever.

*José Froilan 'Pepe' Gonzalez* was born on 5 October 1922 in Arrecifes in Argentina. He developed his control through driving the powerful road racing cars in his home country, and these vehicles - with their poor road-holding capabilities - helped him to control the slides on dirt roads. When he appeared on the Grand Prix circuit his technique seemed to be to throw the car at the corners as fast as possible, counteracting the slides with his large, powerful arms. The son of a Chevrolet dealer near Buenos Aires, Gonzalez was a remarkable athlete despite his stout frame. He was a fine swimmer and cyclist, a good rifle shot and, like his compatriot Fangio, a production car road racer. By 1949 he joined Fangio on a European tour which led to a drive for Ferrari in 1951 at Reims for the French Grand Prix. Gonzalez got as high as second place before having to hand over the car to team leader Ascari. He stayed with the Italian team for the rest of the year, winning his first Grand Prix at Silverstone, which was the first world championship win for Ferrari. 'El Cabezon' (Fat Head) - as he was christened by his countrymen - went on to drive for Maserati in 1952 and 1953 before returning to Ferrari in 1954, again winning at Silverstone, where he beat the powerful Mercedes. He took second place in the world championship and won the Le Mans 24 hour race co-driving with Maurice Trintignant. His career received a setback when he crashed whilst practicing for the 1954 TT race at Dundrod, breaking his shoulder and he decided to retire from full-time racing. However, he raced in a further four Grands Prix, including the race in 1956 at Silverstone, where he was affectionately known as 'The Pampas Bull'. He got no further than the starting line when a driveshaft joint broke. Gonzalez raced in his final Grand Prix in 1960 at Buenos Aires, where he finished tenth in a Ferrari. He then chose to concentrate on his garage business in Argentina.

## Grand Prix Wins

*1951*
**Britain**
*1954*
**Britain**

# 45

## Wolfgang von Trips

> **"** It could happen tomorrow. That's the thing about this business. You never know. **"**

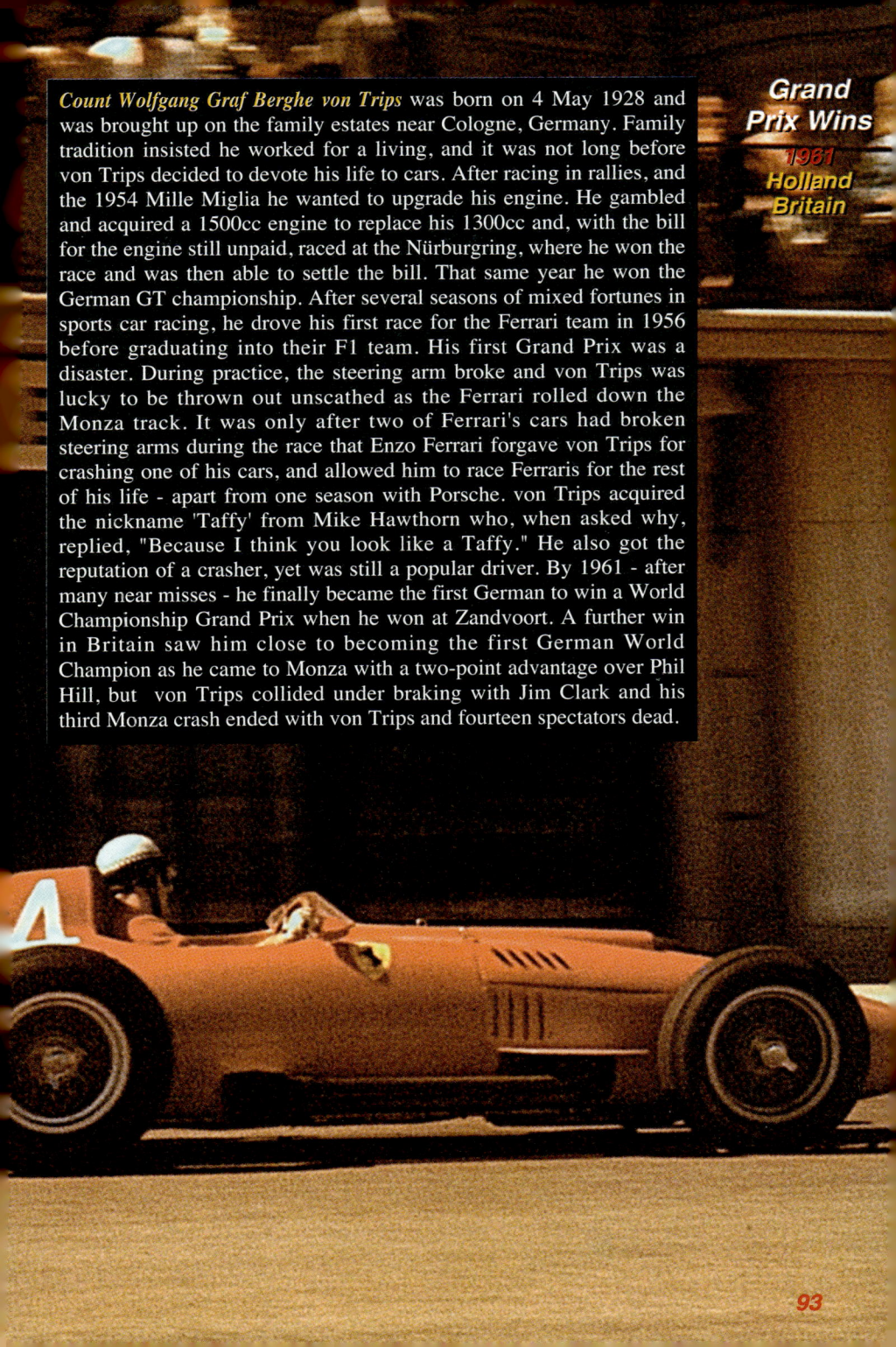

*Count Wolfgang Graf Berghe von Trips* was born on 4 May 1928 and was brought up on the family estates near Cologne, Germany. Family tradition insisted he worked for a living, and it was not long before von Trips decided to devote his life to cars. After racing in rallies, and the 1954 Mille Miglia he wanted to upgrade his engine. He gambled and acquired a 1500cc engine to replace his 1300cc and, with the bill for the engine still unpaid, raced at the Nürburgring, where he won the race and was then able to settle the bill. That same year he won the German GT championship. After several seasons of mixed fortunes in sports car racing, he drove his first race for the Ferrari team in 1956 before graduating into their F1 team. His first Grand Prix was a disaster. During practice, the steering arm broke and von Trips was lucky to be thrown out unscathed as the Ferrari rolled down the Monza track. It was only after two of Ferrari's cars had broken steering arms during the race that Enzo Ferrari forgave von Trips for crashing one of his cars, and allowed him to race Ferraris for the rest of his life - apart from one season with Porsche. von Trips acquired the nickname 'Taffy' from Mike Hawthorn who, when asked why, replied, "Because I think you look like a Taffy." He also got the reputation of a crasher, yet was still a popular driver. By 1961 - after many near misses - he finally became the first German to win a World Championship Grand Prix when he won at Zandvoort. A further win in Britain saw him close to becoming the first German World Champion as he came to Monza with a two-point advantage over Phil Hill, but von Trips collided under braking with Jim Clark and his third Monza crash ended with von Trips and fourteen spectators dead.

## Grand Prix Wins

**1961**
Holland
Britain

# 46

" Style is *very* important. It's the manner in which you conduct yourself, a means of achieving things, the way you handle yourself. "

## Peter Revson

*Peter Jeffrey Revson* was born on 27 February 1939 in New York and after studying mechanical engineering at Cornell University and Liberal Arts at Columbia, he started to move towards market research as a career. Revson began racing as a hobby but in 1962 formed Revson-Mayer Formula Junior team with Teddy Mayer, later to become team boss at McLaren, and soon Revson became a full-time racing driver. It was assumed that Revson had unlimited wealth, but the family fortune through the Revlon cosmetics empire did not come his way and he was forced to rely on the money he earnt. He came to Europe in 1963 and two years later he won the F3 race at Monaco and substituted for Jim Clark in the Lotus F2 car whenever possible. Revson returned to the States to compete in Can-Am and sedan racing, and continued with his racing career despite the death of his brother Doug whilst racing in Denmark. Revson's family strongly disapproved of racing, and Peter's insistence on pursuing his chosen career caused a rift within the family. In 1969 Revson drove a Brabham at Indianapolis, finishing fifth, which led to Carl Haas giving him a Can-Am Lola drive and he soon became America's road racing hero. In 1971 he won the Can-Am series in Bruce McLaren's car after the New Zealander's death the previous year. Revson then drove for the McLaren F1 team in 1972 and 1973, partnering the man he beat to the Can-Am title, Denny Hulme. In both seasons he finished fifth in the world championship, yet became more famous for dating the 1973 Miss World, Marjorie Wallace, than for his performances on the track. He made a surprise move to Shadow in 1974, but was tragically killed on 22 March whilst testing for the forthcoming South African Grand Prix. As he approached the tricky Barbecue bend at Kyalami, his front suspension broke and he crashed into the barriers at high speed, dying instantly.

## Grand Prix Wins

**1973**
Britain
Canada

**47**

" I have always been interested in the mathematics of racing. If something works well or even, if it doesn't, I like to know exactly why. I cannot just accept things without understanding them as well. "

*Jean-Pierre Jabouille*

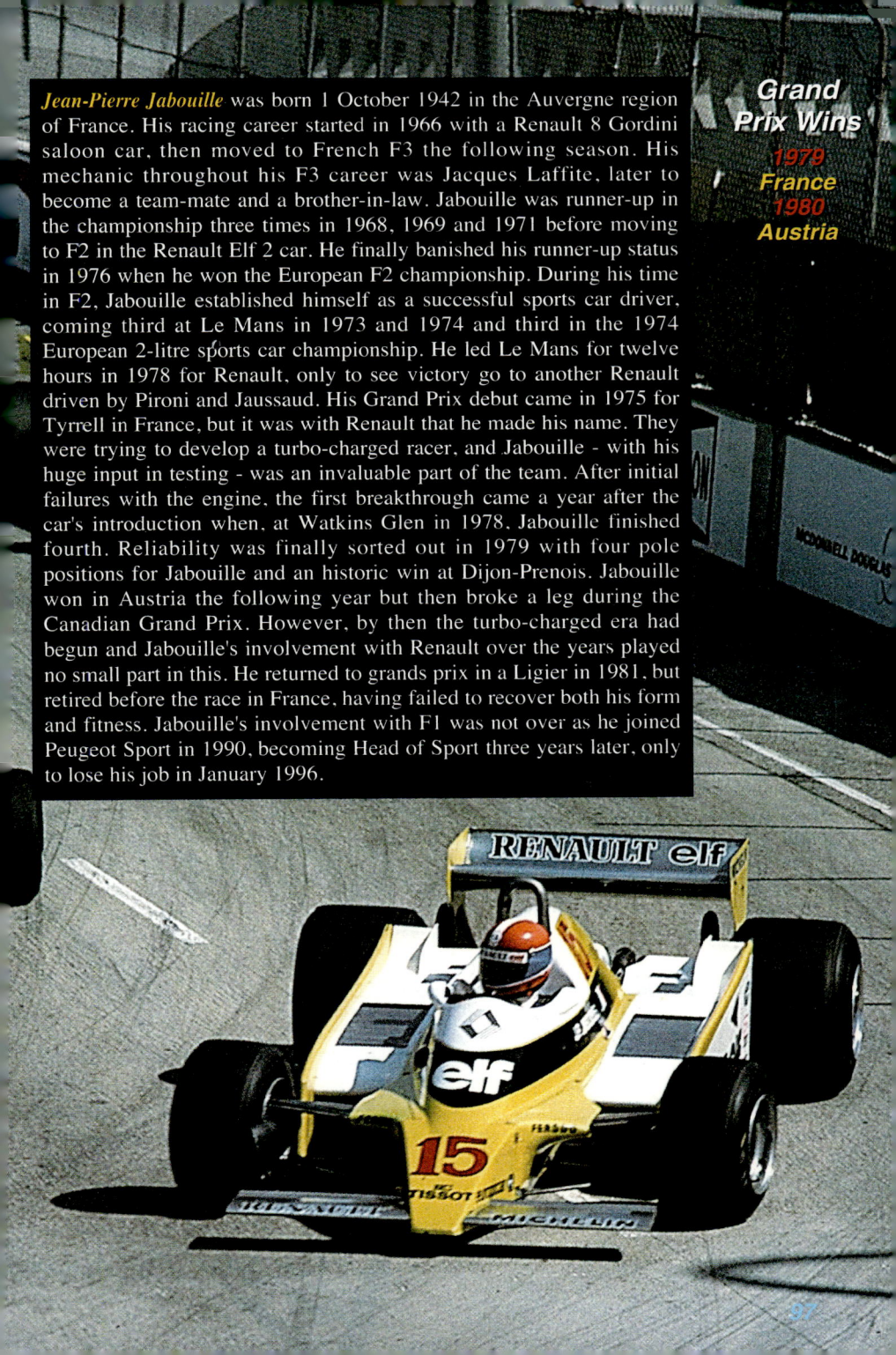

*Jean-Pierre Jabouille* was born 1 October 1942 in the Auvergne region of France. His racing career started in 1966 with a Renault 8 Gordini saloon car, then moved to French F3 the following season. His mechanic throughout his F3 career was Jacques Laffite, later to become a team-mate and a brother-in-law. Jabouille was runner-up in the championship three times in 1968, 1969 and 1971 before moving to F2 in the Renault Elf 2 car. He finally banished his runner-up status in 1976 when he won the European F2 championship. During his time in F2, Jabouille established himself as a successful sports car driver, coming third at Le Mans in 1973 and 1974 and third in the 1974 European 2-litre sports car championship. He led Le Mans for twelve hours in 1978 for Renault, only to see victory go to another Renault driven by Pironi and Jaussaud. His Grand Prix debut came in 1975 for Tyrrell in France, but it was with Renault that he made his name. They were trying to develop a turbo-charged racer, and Jabouille - with his huge input in testing - was an invaluable part of the team. After initial failures with the engine, the first breakthrough came a year after the car's introduction when, at Watkins Glen in 1978, Jabouille finished fourth. Reliability was finally sorted out in 1979 with four pole positions for Jabouille and an historic win at Dijon-Prenois. Jabouille won in Austria the following year but then broke a leg during the Canadian Grand Prix. However, by then the turbo-charged era had begun and Jabouille's involvement with Renault over the years played no small part in this. He returned to grands prix in a Ligier in 1981, but retired before the race in France, having failed to recover both his form and fitness. Jabouille's involvement with F1 was not over as he joined Peugeot Sport in 1990, becoming Head of Sport three years later, only to lose his job in January 1996.

## Grand Prix Wins

*1979*
*France*
*1980*
*Austria*

# 48

## Pedro Rodriguez

> "You can play around there (Monaco), slide the car and have fun, but I prefer somewhere like Spa. There you cannot make a mistake and be safe, you know. You have to race really precise..."

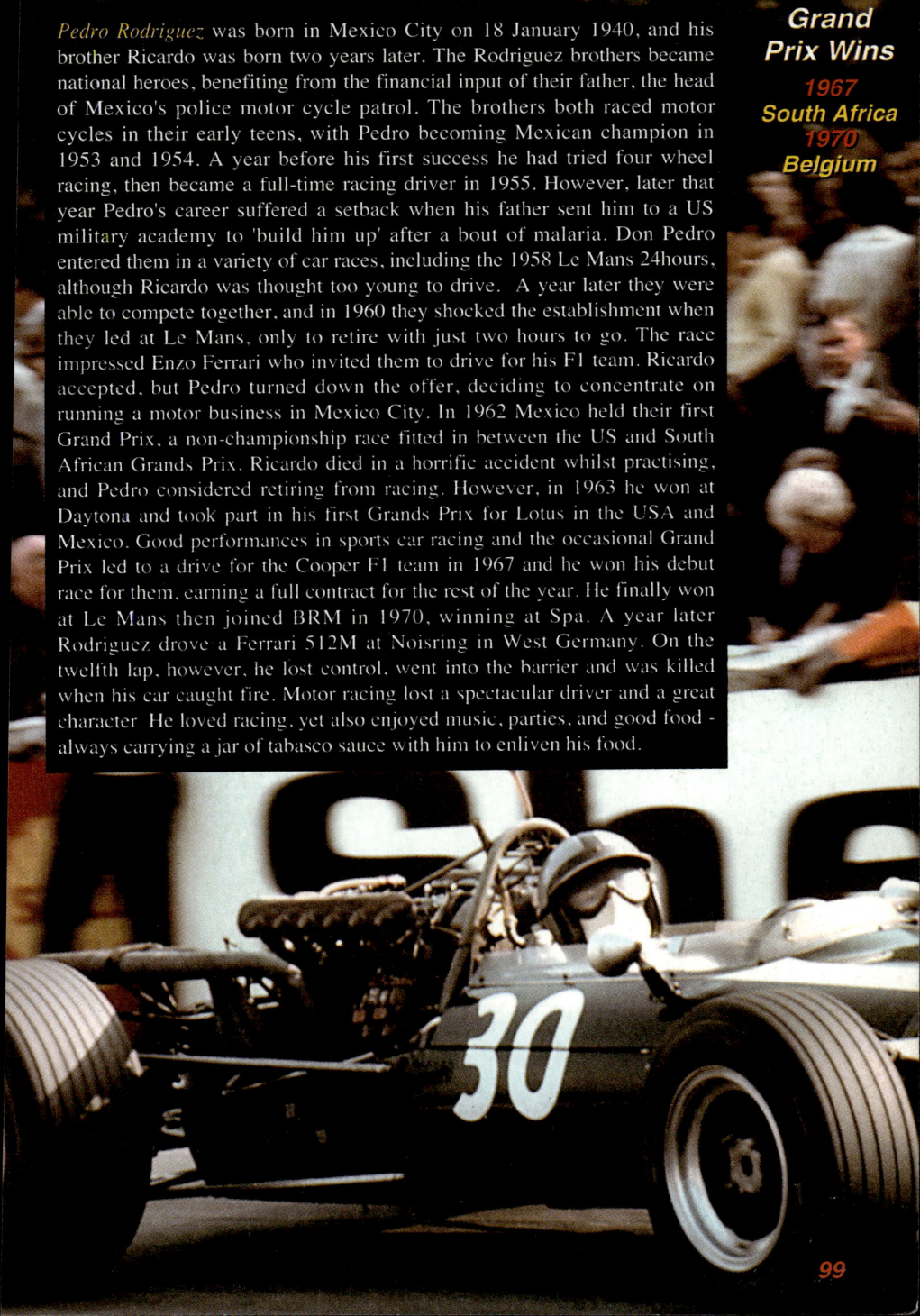

*Pedro Rodriguez* was born in Mexico City on 18 January 1940, and his brother Ricardo was born two years later. The Rodriguez brothers became national heroes, benefiting from the financial input of their father, the head of Mexico's police motor cycle patrol. The brothers both raced motor cycles in their early teens, with Pedro becoming Mexican champion in 1953 and 1954. A year before his first success he had tried four wheel racing, then became a full-time racing driver in 1955. However, later that year Pedro's career suffered a setback when his father sent him to a US military academy to 'build him up' after a bout of malaria. Don Pedro entered them in a variety of car races, including the 1958 Le Mans 24hours, although Ricardo was thought too young to drive. A year later they were able to compete together, and in 1960 they shocked the establishment when they led at Le Mans, only to retire with just two hours to go. The race impressed Enzo Ferrari who invited them to drive for his F1 team. Ricardo accepted, but Pedro turned down the offer, deciding to concentrate on running a motor business in Mexico City. In 1962 Mexico held their first Grand Prix, a non-championship race fitted in between the US and South African Grands Prix. Ricardo died in a horrific accident whilst practising, and Pedro considered retiring from racing. However, in 1963 he won at Daytona and took part in his first Grands Prix for Lotus in the USA and Mexico. Good performances in sports car racing and the occasional Grand Prix led to a drive for the Cooper F1 team in 1967 and he won his debut race for them, earning a full contract for the rest of the year. He finally won at Le Mans then joined BRM in 1970, winning at Spa. A year later Rodriguez drove a Ferrari 512M at Noisring in West Germany. On the twelfth lap, however, he lost control, went into the barrier and was killed when his car caught fire. Motor racing lost a spectacular driver and a great character. He loved racing, yet also enjoyed music, parties, and good food - always carrying a jar of tabasco sauce with him to enliven his food.

## Grand Prix Wins

**1967 South Africa**
**1970 Belgium**

*49*

*Johnny Herbert*

" I think every driver, whether they win a Grand Prix or they don't, feels that they can do more. If you win ten grands prix, you still probably think it should have been twenty, or if you win twenty you think it should be thirty. You're always going to think you can achieve more."

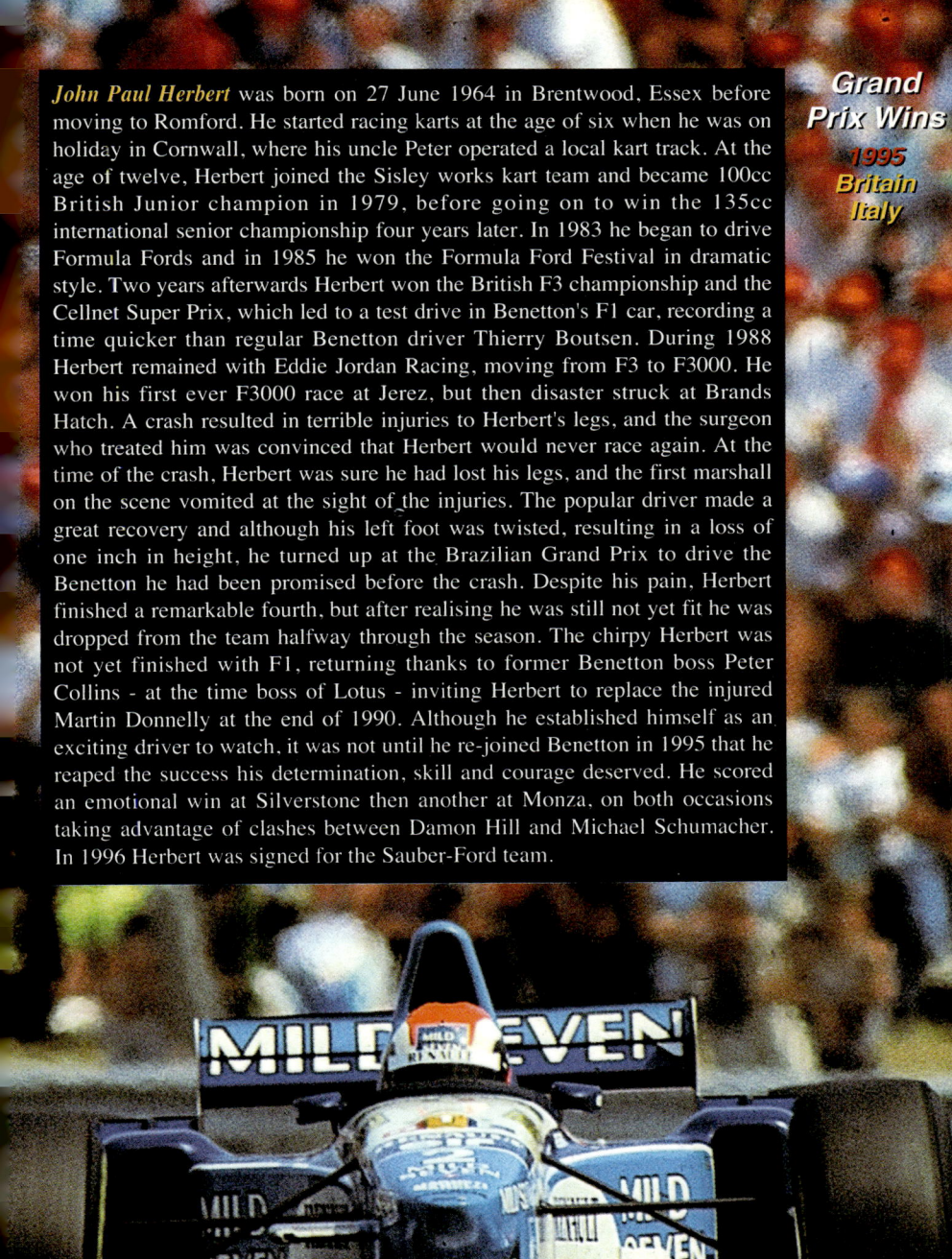

*John Paul Herbert* was born on 27 June 1964 in Brentwood, Essex before moving to Romford. He started racing karts at the age of six when he was on holiday in Cornwall, where his uncle Peter operated a local kart track. At the age of twelve, Herbert joined the Sisley works kart team and became 100cc British Junior champion in 1979, before going on to win the 135cc international senior championship four years later. In 1983 he began to drive Formula Fords and in 1985 he won the Formula Ford Festival in dramatic style. Two years afterwards Herbert won the British F3 championship and the Cellnet Super Prix, which led to a test drive in Benetton's F1 car, recording a time quicker than regular Benetton driver Thierry Boutsen. During 1988 Herbert remained with Eddie Jordan Racing, moving from F3 to F3000. He won his first ever F3000 race at Jerez, but then disaster struck at Brands Hatch. A crash resulted in terrible injuries to Herbert's legs, and the surgeon who treated him was convinced that Herbert would never race again. At the time of the crash, Herbert was sure he had lost his legs, and the first marshall on the scene vomited at the sight of the injuries. The popular driver made a great recovery and although his left foot was twisted, resulting in a loss of one inch in height, he turned up at the Brazilian Grand Prix to drive the Benetton he had been promised before the crash. Despite his pain, Herbert finished a remarkable fourth, but after realising he was still not yet fit he was dropped from the team halfway through the season. The chirpy Herbert was not yet finished with F1, returning thanks to former Benetton boss Peter Collins - at the time boss of Lotus - inviting Herbert to replace the injured Martin Donnelly at the end of 1990. Although he established himself as an exciting driver to watch, it was not until he re-joined Benetton in 1995 that he reaped the success his determination, skill and courage deserved. He scored an emotional win at Silverstone then another at Monza, on both occasions taking advantage of clashes between Damon Hill and Michael Schumacher. In 1996 Herbert was signed for the Sauber-Ford team.

## Grand Prix Wins

*1995*
*Britain*
*Italy*

# 50

## Patrick Depailler

" I run all the time at the limit. I *like* to run at the limit, to push things as far as I can. I am the same at everything. If I decide to do something I give it everything. All the time. "

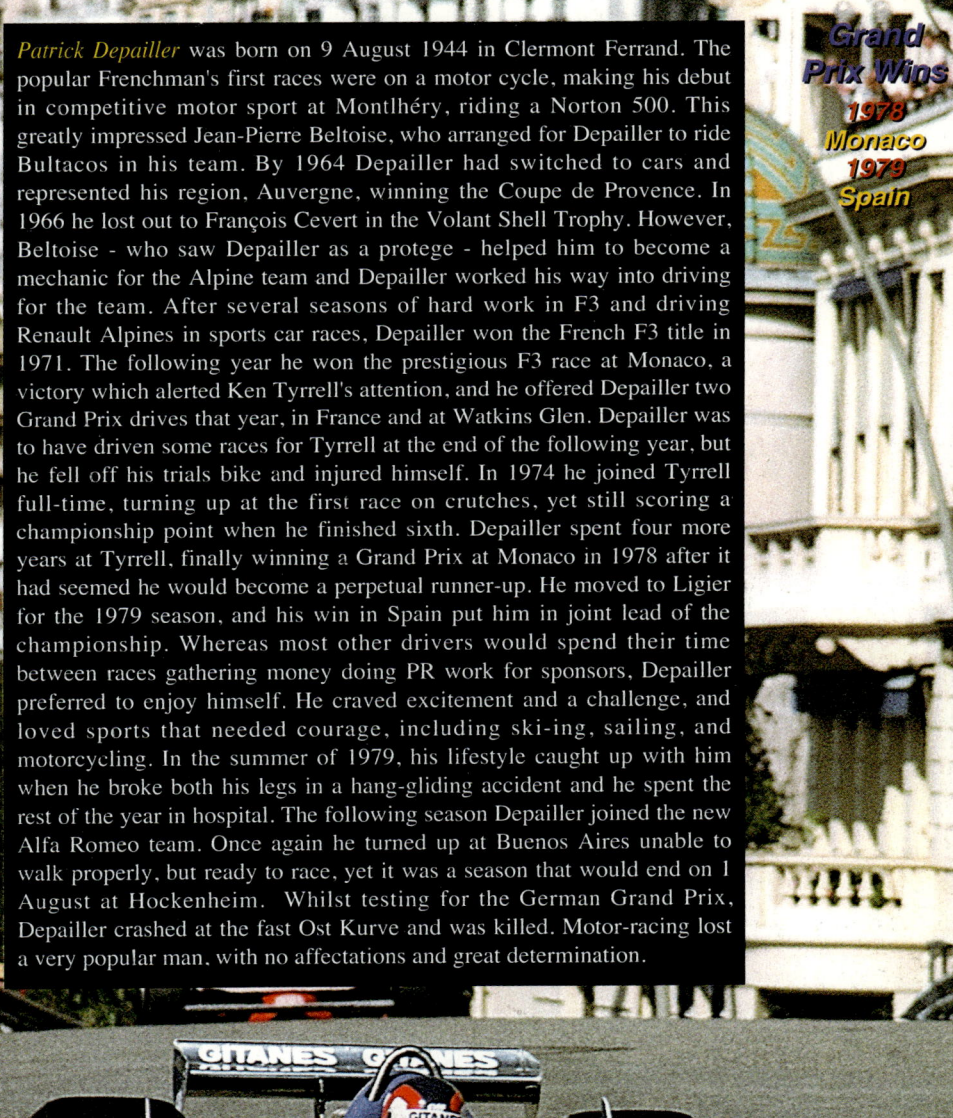

*Patrick Depailler* was born on 9 August 1944 in Clermont Ferrand. The popular Frenchman's first races were on a motor cycle, making his debut in competitive motor sport at Montlhéry, riding a Norton 500. This greatly impressed Jean-Pierre Beltoise, who arranged for Depailler to ride Bultacos in his team. By 1964 Depailler had switched to cars and represented his region, Auvergne, winning the Coupe de Provence. In 1966 he lost out to François Cevert in the Volant Shell Trophy. However, Beltoise - who saw Depailler as a protege - helped him to become a mechanic for the Alpine team and Depailler worked his way into driving for the team. After several seasons of hard work in F3 and driving Renault Alpines in sports car races, Depailler won the French F3 title in 1971. The following year he won the prestigious F3 race at Monaco, a victory which alerted Ken Tyrrell's attention, and he offered Depailler two Grand Prix drives that year, in France and at Watkins Glen. Depailler was to have driven some races for Tyrrell at the end of the following year, but he fell off his trials bike and injured himself. In 1974 he joined Tyrrell full-time, turning up at the first race on crutches, yet still scoring a championship point when he finished sixth. Depailler spent four more years at Tyrrell, finally winning a Grand Prix at Monaco in 1978 after it had seemed he would become a perpetual runner-up. He moved to Ligier for the 1979 season, and his win in Spain put him in joint lead of the championship. Whereas most other drivers would spend their time between races gathering money doing PR work for sponsors, Depailler preferred to enjoy himself. He craved excitement and a challenge, and loved sports that needed courage, including ski-ing, sailing, and motorcycling. In the summer of 1979, his lifestyle caught up with him when he broke both his legs in a hang-gliding accident and he spent the rest of the year in hospital. The following season Depailler joined the new Alfa Romeo team. Once again he turned up at Buenos Aires unable to walk properly, but ready to race, yet it was a season that would end on 1 August at Hockenheim. Whilst testing for the German Grand Prix, Depailler crashed at the fast Ost Kurve and was killed. Motor-racing lost a very popular man, with no affectations and great determination.

**Grand Prix Wins**
*1978 Monaco*
*1979 Spain*

## WORLD CHAMPIONSHIP TITLES

| Year | Driver | Constructor |
|------|--------|-------------|
| 1950 | Giuseppe Farina | Alfa Romeo |
| 1951 | Juan-Manuel Fangio | Alfa Romeo |
| 1952 | Alberto Ascari | Ferrari |
| 1953 | Alberto Ascari | Ferrari |
| 1954 | Juan-Manuel Fangio | Maserati/Mercedes |
| 1955 | Juan-Manuel Fangio | Mercedes |
| 1956 | Juan-Manuel Fangio | Lancia-Ferrari |
| 1957 | Juan-Manuel Fangio | Maserati |
| 1958 | Mike Hawthorn | Ferrari |
| 1959 | Jack Brabham | Cooper |
| 1960 | Jack Brabham | Cooper |
| 1961 | Phil Hill | Ferrari |
| 1962 | Graham Hill | BRM |
| 1963 | Jim Clark | Lotus |
| 1964 | John Surtees | Ferrari |
| 1965 | Jim Clark | Lotus |
| 1966 | Jack Brabham | Brabham |
| 1967 | Denny Hulme | Brabham |
| 1968 | Graham Hill | Lotus |
| 1969 | Jackie Stewart | Matra |
| 1970 | Jochen Rindt | Lotus |
| 1971 | Jackie Stewart | Tyrrell |
| 1972 | Emerson Fittipaldi | Lotus |
| 1973 | Jackie Stewart | Tyrrell |
| 1974 | Emerson Fittipaldi | McLaren |
| 1975 | Niki Lauda | Ferrari |
| 1976 | James Hunt | McLaren |
| 1977 | Niki Lauda | Ferrari |
| 1978 | Mario Andretti | Lotus |
| 1979 | Jody Scheckter | Ferrari |
| 1980 | Alan Jones | Williams |
| 1981 | Nelson Piquet | Brabham |
| 1982 | Keke Rosberg | Williams |
| 1983 | Nelson Piquet | Brabham |
| 1984 | Niki Lauda | McLaren |
| 1985 | Alain Prost | McLaren |
| 1986 | Alain Prost | McLaren |
| 1987 | Nelson Piquet | Williams |
| 1988 | Ayrton Senna | McLaren |
| 1989 | Alain Prost | McLaren |
| 1990 | Ayrton Senna | McLaren |
| 1991 | Ayrton Senna | McLaren |
| 1992 | Nigel Mansell | Williams |
| 1993 | Alain Prost | Williams |
| 1994 | Michael Schumacher | Benetton |
| 1995 | Michael Schumacher | Benetton |

## GRAND PRIX WINS

|  |  |
|---|---|
| Alain Prost | 51 |
| Ayrton Senna | 41 |
| Nigel Mansell | 31 |
| Jackie Stewart | 27 |
| Jim Clark | 25 |
| Niki Lauda | 25 |
| Juan-Manuel Fangio | 24 |
| Nelson Piquet | 23 |
| Michael Schumacher | 19 |
| Stirling Moss | 16 |
| Jack Brabham | 14 |
| Emerson Fittipaldi | 14 |
| Graham Hill | 14 |
| Alberto Ascari | 13 |
| Damon Hill | 13 |
| Mario Andretti | 12 |
| Alan Jones | 12 |
| Carlos Reutemann | 12 |
| James Hunt | 10 |
| Ronnie Peterson | 10 |
| Jody Scheckter | 10 |
| Gerhard Berger | 9 |
| Denny Hulme | 8 |
| Jacky Ickx | 8 |
| René Arnoux | 7 |
| Tony Brooks | 6 |
| Jacques Laffite | 6 |
| Riccardo Patrese | 6 |
| Jochen Rindt | 6 |
| John Surtees | 6 |
| Gilles Villeneuve | 6 |
| Michele Alboreto | 5 |
| Giuseppe Farina | 5 |
| Clay Regazzoni | 5 |
| Keke Rosberg | 5 |
| John Watson | 5 |
| Dan Gurney | 4 |
| Bruce McLaren | 4 |
| Thierry Boutsen | 3 |
| Peter Collins | 3 |
| Mike Hawthorn | 3 |
| Phil Hill | 3 |
| Didier Pironi | 3 |
| Patrick Depailler | 2 |
| Froilan Gonzalez | 2 |
| Johnny Herbert | 2 |
| Jean-Pierre Jabouille | 2 |
| Peter Revson | 2 |
| Pedro Rodriguez | 2 |
| Wolfgang von Trips | 2 |

## NUMBER OF WINS IN A SEASON

| Driver | Wins | Year | Grands Prix |
|---|---|---|---|
| Nigel Mansell | 9 | 1992 | 16 |
| Michael Schumacher | 9 | 1995 | 17 |
| Ayrton Senna | 8 | 1988 | 16 |
| Michael Schumacher | 8 | 1994 | 16 |
| Alain Prost | 7 | 1984 | 16 |
| Alain Prost | 7 | 1988 | 16 |
| Alain Prost | 7 | 1993 | 16 |
| Jim Clark | 7 | 1963 | 10 |
| Ayrton Senna | 7 | 1991 | 16 |
| Jackie Stewart | 6 | 1969 | 11 |
| Jackie Stewart | 6 | 1971 | 11 |
| Ayrton Senna | 6 | 1989 | 16 |
| Ayrton Senna | 6 | 1990 | 16 |
| Alberto Ascari | 6 | 1952 | 8 |
| Juan-Manuel Fangio | 6 | 1954 | 9 |
| Jim Clark | 6 | 1965 | 10 |
| James Hunt | 6 | 1976 | 16 |
| Mario Andretti | 6 | 1978 | 16 |
| Nigel Mansell | 6 | 1987 | 16 |
| Damon Hill | 6 | 1994 | 16 |
| Niki Lauda | 5 | 1975 | 14 |
| Niki Lauda | 5 | 1976 | 16 |
| Niki Lauda | 5 | 1984 | 16 |
| Alain Prost | 5 | 1985 | 16 |
| Alain Prost | 5 | 1990 | 16 |
| Nigel Mansell | 5 | 1986 | 16 |
| Nigel Mansell | 5 | 1991 | 16 |
| Alberto Ascari | 5 | 1953 | 9 |
| Jack Brabham | 5 | 1960 | 10 |
| Jochen Rindt | 5 | 1970 | 13 |
| Emerson Fittipaldi | 5 | 1972 | 12 |
| Jackie Stewart | 5 | 1973 | 15 |
| Alan Jones | 5 | 1980 | 14 |
| Ayrton Senna | 5 | 1993 | 16 |

## NUMBER OF POLE POSITIONS

| | |
|---|---|
| Ayrton Senna | 65 |
| Jim Clark | 33 |
| Alain Prost | 33 |
| Nigel Mansell | 32 |
| Juan-Manuel Fangio | 29 |
| Niki Lauda | 24 |
| Nelson Piquet | 24 |
| Mario Andretti | 18 |
| René Arnoux | 18 |
| Jackie Stewart | 17 |
| Stirling Moss | 16 |
| Alberto Ascari | 14 |
| James Hunt | 14 |
| Ronnie Peterson | 14 |
| Jack Brabham | 13 |
| Graham Hill | 13 |
| Jacky Ickx | 13 |
| Gerhard Berger | 11 |
| Damon Hill | 11 |
| Jochen Rindt | 10 |
| Michael Schumacher | 10 |

## BIBLIOGRAPHY

### MAGAZINES & ANNUALS
*Autosport* (various issues) [Haymarket Specialist Motoring Magazines Ltd.]
*Motor Sport* (various issues) [Teesdale Publishing Co. Ltd.]
*GP News* (various issues) [Peakcourt Ltd.]
*Grand Prix International* (various issues) [GELT]
*Autocourse* (various years) [Hazleton Publishing]
*Automobile Sport 81-82* [Iconplan Ltd.]
*Automobile Sport 82-83* [Superprofile Ltd.]
*Automobile Sport 83-85* [Tenorhart Ltd.]
*FIA Formula One World Championship Yearbook 1989* [Virgin Books]
*FIA Formula One World Championship Yearbook 1990* [Piccadilly Promotion Ltd.]
*Formula One FOCA Yearbooks 1987 & 1988* [Grid Publishing]

### BOOKS
*British Grand Prix* by Maurice Hamilton [The Crowood Press] 1989
*Champion Year* by Mike Hawthorn [William Kimber & Co. Ltd.] 1959
*Chequered Flag* by Ivan Rendall [George Weidenfeld & Nicolson Ltd.] 1993
*Damon Hill - From Zero To Hero* by Alan Henry [Haynes] 1994
*Designs on Victory - On the Grand Prix Trail with Benetton* by Derick Allsop [Stanley Paul & Co. Ltd.] 1993
*Formula One - Driver by Driver* by Alan Henry [The Crowood Press] 1992
*Gerhard Berger - The Human Face of Formula One* by Christopher Hilton [Patrick Stephens Ltd.] 1993

*Graham* by Graham Hill with Neil Ewart [Arrow Books] 1977
*Grand Prix! 1950-1965* by Mike Lang [Haynes Publishing Group] 1981
*Grand Prix* by Trevor R.Griffiths [Bloomsbury Publishing Ltd.] 1992
*Grand Prix Book of Motor Racing Quotes* by Eugene Weber [Hodder & Stoughton] 1995
*Grand Prix Greats* by Nigel Roebuck [Patrick StephensLtd.] 1986
*Grand Prix Requiem* by William Court [Patrick Stephens Ltd.] 1992
*Grand Prix Winners* by Denis Jenkinson, Nigel Roebuck, Alan Henry, Maurice Hamilton, Steve Small [Hazleton Publishing] 1995
*Guinness Guide To International Motor Racing* by Peter Higham [Guinness Publishing Ltd.] 1995
*James Hunt* by Gerald Donaldson [Collins Willow] 1994
*Keke* by Keke Rosberg and Keith Botsford [Stanley Paul & Co. Ltd.] 1985
*Kimberley Racing Driver Profiles: Niki Lauda* by Alan Henry [Kimberley's] 1986
*Kimberley Racing Driver Profiles: Nelson Piquet* by Ric Van Kempen [Kimberley's] 1984
*Kimberley Racing Driver Profiles: Keke Rosberg* by Bob Constanduros [Kimberley's] 1984
*Life at the Limit* by Graham Hill [Pan Books] 1971
*Life in the Fast Lane* by Alain Prost with Jean Louis Moncet [Stanley Paul & Co. Ltd.] 1989
*Michael Schumacher* by Christopher Hilton [Patrick Stephens Ltd.] 1994
*Observers Book of Motor Sport* by Graham Macbeth [Frederick Warne] 1978
*Stirling Moss: My Cars, My Career* by Stirling Moss and Doug Nye [Patrick Stephens Ltd.] 1987
*The Fast Ones* by Peter Miller [Stanley Paul] 1962
*Williams Renault Formula One Racing Book* by Xavier Chimits and Francois Granet [Dorling Kindersley] 1994
*Winners* by Brian Laban [Orbis Publishing] 1981

# Forthcoming

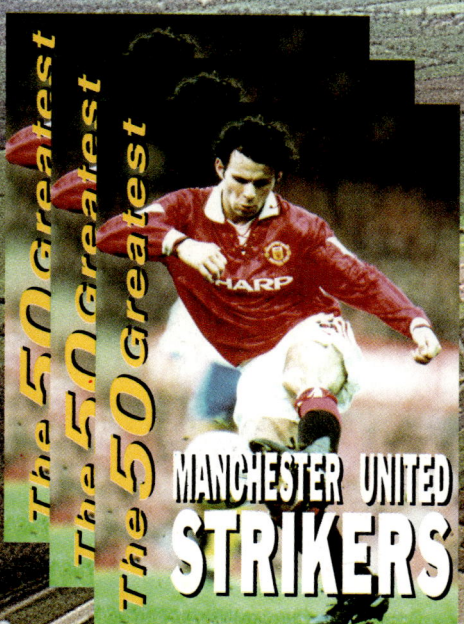

From Best to Charlton, from Law to Coppell, from Cantona to Giggs, they're all here in this magnificent book - Manchester United's 50 Greatest Strikers throughout more than 100 years of Manchester United FC

**£8.99**

**MANCHESTER UNITED STRIKERS**

From Rush to Dalglish, from Hunt to Keegan and from Toshack to Fowler, they're all here in this magnificent book - Liverpool's 50 Greatest Strikers throughout more than 100 years of Liverpool FC history

**£8.99**

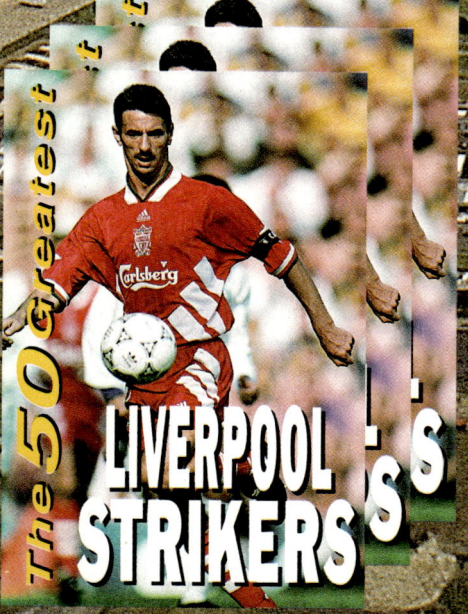

**LIVERPOOL STRIKERS**

# Titles

From Christie to Gunnell, from Jesse Owens to Seb Coe, from Ovett to Cram - they're all here, the 50 Greatest Athletes of all time.

**£8.99**

Available from

**CHAMPION PRESS**

P.O. Box 284, Sidcup, Kent DA15 8JY
0181-302-6446

The 50 Greatest **ATHLETES**

The 50 Greatest **RUGBY UNION STARS**

From Gareth Edwards to JPR Williams, from Willie John McBride to Bill Beaumont, from Will Carling and David Campese to Gavin Hastings - they are all here, The 50 Greatest Rugby Union stars of all time.

**£8.99**